TEACH A KID TO SAVE

TEACH
A KiD
TO SAVE

A FUN, HANDS-ON APPROACH TO BUILDING SMART MONEY HABITS

STEPHEN DAY

R Revell

a division of Baker Publishing Group
Grand Rapids, Michigan

© 2026 by Stephen Harlan Day

Published by Revell
a division of Baker Publishing Group
Grand Rapids, Michigan
RevellBooks.com

Printed in the United States of America

Library of Congress Cataloging-in-Publication Data
Names: Day, Stephen H. (Stephen Harlan) author
Title: Teach a kid to save : a fun, hands-on approach to building smart money habits / Stephen Day.
Description: Grand Rapids, Michigan : Revell, [2026] | Includes bibliographical references.
Identifiers: LCCN 2025020569 | ISBN 9780800747534 (paperback) | ISBN 9780800747848 (casebound) | ISBN 9781493452675 (ebook)
Subjects: LCSH: Financial literacy—Study and teaching | Children—Finance, Personal | Parenting
Classification: LCC HG179 .D3676 2026 | DDC 332.024—dc23/eng/20250703
LC record available at https://lccn.loc.gov/2025020569

Cover design by Christopher Gilbert, Studio Gearbox

The author is represented by WordServe Literary Group, www.wordserveliterary.com.

Baker Publishing Group publications use paper produced from sustainable forestry practices and postconsumer waste whenever possible.

26 27 28 29 30 31 32   7 6 5 4 3 2 1

FOR MOM AND DAD

CONTENTS

FOREWORD

Some years ago, when I was still relatively new to Richmond, Virginia, I had the honor of being introduced to a group of college students by Stephen Day. He was generous and kind, lending me his credibility at the university where he worked. Now I'm delighted to have the chance to return the favor.

Stephen has written a wonderful book about teaching children what money is—how to use it, how to work for it, and so much more. It's fun to read (I got so engrossed, I read it in one sitting!) and deeply practical. But for me, it's especially meaningful because I've had the privilege of seeing much of it lived out. We live just a few blocks from Stephen and his family, and our kids share classes, bike rides, sports teams, and playdates. I've seen the fruit of his teaching firsthand—even in the form of a small cardboard statue created by one of his children for their family's mini-economy.

In short: It works. The principles and practices in this book aren't just wise—they're effective. My wife, Lauren, even created a small household store inspired by Stephen's ideas. But I won't try to summarize what's better experienced through his words.

Instead, I'll simply return the favor: Let me introduce you to Stephen Day—a marvelous father, a thoughtful writer, and someone you'll learn a great deal from.

Justin Whitmel Earley, father, business lawyer, and author of *Habits of the Household* and *The Body Teaches the Soul*

INTRODUCTION

"Only if you pay me."

Manuela met her mother Evelyn's eyes as she spoke. Evelyn gaped back at her five-year-old daughter, astonished.

"You were so excited to do your summer play book last week, Manuela!" Evelyn pleaded. "Why don't you want to do it anymore? You can get the sticker at the end if you finish."

"It's not a play book. It's work," insisted the rising kindergartener. "You paid me to do the letters and numbers before! I should get paid for this *work*book. It's *work*."

On this point, Manuela was correct. The "play book" was in fact an enrichment exercise book designed to keep kids engaged with academics over the summer. She was not fooled by her parents' feeble attempt at rebranding.

What should I do? Evelyn wondered. When the first workbook came in the mail, Manuela had been so excited to do it. She had torn through the numbers, letters, and story exercises, pursuing the prize at the end of the chapter: a sticker. But when a new workbook came in the mail the next week, Manuela hadn't been interested this time around, so her parents had paid her a quarter to do it. When the third week of summer brought with it a third workbook,

11

Manuela put her foot down. If last week's work deserved payment, so did this week's. She had learned the value of her work. But not in a way that her parents considered good.

Evelyn pondered her options. Should she threaten a punishment—no screen time until the workbook was done? Or keep the quarters coming? Perhaps give Manuela a raise?

In the end, she did what so many parents do: She gave up. Manuela went back to playing with her toys, and the wonders of learning contained in the workbook were left untouched.

This scenario—the broad strokes of which are likely familiar to you if you have young kids—shows a riot of parental insecurity and confusion. Parents ask, How do we teach our kids about the value of money? Should we pay them if they do chores or academic work? Punish them if they don't? Both? Neither? Shouldn't they just be doing chores to help out around the house because they're part of the family? That's what we did when we were kids, and we never complained! (Right?)

If we don't pay them, how can we teach them the connection between work and money? How will they get money? So many parents desperately want to teach their kids the basics of personal finance, but they don't know where to start.

◼ ◼ ◼ ◼

Teach a Kid to Save helps parents sift through the swirl of conflicting advice about money and work. It recognizes the tension between different motivational styles when it comes to getting kids to do chores and proposes a simple system that makes these complicated choices easy—or at least easier. This system is not about managing chores, though it does do that. The chores are a side benefit. It teaches kids about money, work, and goals, and how all these things connect.

This system is called a mini-economy.

On the surface, a mini-economy looks like a way to organize chores, allowance, budgeting, and spending. However, its purpose is more ambitious than that. It is about *teaching*—not just managing—kids as they learn about money, work, and life. Elementary-age children can learn financial habits and values. A mini-economy is an easy on-ramp to get parents and children talking and learning about these vitally important life skills. It's about giving kids the basic tools they need to take charge of their financial lives as they grow.

In a mini-economy, kids earn play money, which they budget into categories of giving, saving, and spending. Then they have an opportunity to spend their money in a household store that you set up on the kitchen table. Finally, they create businesses to make goods and services to sell to siblings and parents in the store—parents must also earn mini-economy money, you see. This might sound complicated, but as you'll see in the coming chapters, it's actually quite simple. You can even do it as a short, fun summer project. Once you're up and running, the benefits will touch every aspect of your family life.

A mini-economy is just that: a small *economy*, or system for making choices about producing and consuming things. It's different from a traditional top-down method of parents paying kids for chores. In the traditional way, money comes straight from the parents and goes straight to the toy section at Target. It's a management tool. But in a mini-economy, the money *circulates* through the house. The kids can see how it flows. They see the connection between their work, their saving and spending choices, their siblings' saving and spending choices, and their parents' saving and spending choices. This interconnection of money, work, and each person's goals helps kids learn the value of things. It doesn't just show them how to work with money; it shows them how money works.

I'm trying to help you avoid having this interaction with your kids ever again:

"Mommy, can we buy this?"

"No, honey."

"Mommy, can we buy that?"

"No."

"Mommy . . ."

"NO!"

Is this what we want our children's first memories of spending choices to be? No! It's a bad experience for Mommy and makes her feel tightfisted and grumpy. It's not a good experience for children either, even if their parents cave in and buy them what they want. This is because they learn the way to get things is to badger their parents, and whether or not they get what they want is based on their parents' moods.

This is not a good way to introduce children to spending decisions. As far as children are concerned, money choices often come down to one thing: *Is Mom or Dad feeling nice right now, or mean? Nice means they'll buy me what I want. Mean means they won't.* This kind of interaction teaches kids the wrong lessons about the things we buy.

Adults are uncomfortable teaching their children about money for several reasons. First, parents might not have the knowledge—the words—to communicate clearly and might even have taboos against talking about something as private as money.

But there are other difficulties. Usually we teach our kids how to do things by modeling—we show them how to do things and guide them along the way. We model how to read, wash dishes, play basketball, and so forth. But parents earn far more money than children do. How can we demonstrate how to use money when our financial decisions are on another level from theirs?

Kids need lots of practice if they are to master a skill. However, they don't get enough opportunities to practice with money. Sure, they may get some practice with buying decisions and sometimes even saving decisions. But what about making decisions as a *producer*, someone who makes important choices about what to produce, and how that connects with the money they make?

Kids can reach adulthood with some practice as consumers but usually not as producers.

If only there was a way to have these conversations in a way that works for both parents and children! There is, of course, which is why you are reading this.

▪ ▪ ▪ ▪

When I first started a play-money economy in my own home, I thought the goal was to teach my children about money. But I quickly found out it was something more: I was teaching them about life and the big world of human society. I was trying to connect our family's values with the fraught domain of working and spending.

I didn't need a set of rules. I needed a *system*, one that would provide teachable moments; tie together work, money, and our values; and help kids understand the trade-offs people face in their everyday choices.

The word for such a system is an *economy*. The term comes from the ancient Greek word *oikos*, which refers to the management of household wealth in pursuit of worthy goals. A "mini-economy"—a small economy—is an appropriate way to introduce children to the way money flows. They can then locate themselves in the "big economy"—the real world.

I was already deeply familiar with mini-economies. In my day job, I trained schoolteachers on how to teach economics and personal finance to their students. I was experienced in showing elementary school teachers how to implement mini-economies in their classrooms; the system has been in schools for years. I wrote my PhD dissertation on how classroom teachers use mini-economies. I came to learn about them in the first place because my dad, Harlan Day, literally wrote the book on how teachers can create classroom mini-economies. It's called *The Classroom Mini-Economy*. And what's more, he and my mom tested the idea on my three brothers and me when we were children. My parents

15

organized our household tasks using a mini-economy and started a store on our back porch. I was born into this! It was time to put the mini-economy into practice with my own family.

My wife and I started small, very small. We did what countless families have done in the past: We gave the kids household jobs (but with fun job titles!) and paid them in homemade currency. We created a family store in which they could buy privileges, like extra TV time or a solo adventure with Dad (complete with food and with no siblings in tow). We introduced two things they had to do with their money right when they got it, before they bought anything: *taxes* and *giving* (in our case, to church and charity). Then we added a bit more: We taught them how to keep records of their earning and spending and to create their own businesses. They had many opportunities to practice financial choices in a family setting with low stakes. Things began to run more smoothly, we all had fun, and work even got done around the house! We called it our mini-economy at home.

This basic framework was not particularly novel. Like I said, it has all been done before, both at home and in schools. But while we did it, we learned a lot of lessons I thought others should be aware of. There are wrong ways to do a mini-economy, but there are also many opportunities to make it amazing. It helps to know what these are ahead of time, before you mistakenly teach your children something wrong or, on the other hand, miss opportunities for teachable moments.

Please know that this does not need to take over your household life. Rather, it's meant as a way to gamify a portion of it as a teaching tool through which your kids learn the ways money and work interrelate. They gain a sense of broader economic life and their place in it.

Questions abound: Should I use a mini-economy mainly as a method for reward and punishment? (No.) Should I allow children to try to sell things to their neighbors that the neighbors do not want? (Maybe. You'll have to finesse this one. See chapter 9.) Are there special days or times when we do not work or buy things? (In our household, yes.) Each of these questions invites parents to create a framework in which their kids can learn about the world of working and spending in a way that is fun, creative, and allows the family's values to shine through.

◾ ◾ ◾ ◾

There are dozens more specific, practical questions involved in running your mini-economy at home, and we'll get to them. When you do start, you'll be ready to make the most of it. Rather than being an issue that is scary, embarrassing, or boring, learning how to manage money will be something that will resonate with your children. You will be able to teach them in a way that is responsible and fun for everyone.

This book is organized into three parts. Part 1, "Why We Are Doing This," is for readers who really want a deeper understanding of what, when, and how kids should learn about money and work. It deals with the thorny issues and questions that bedevil parents as they begin teaching their children about money and work. Part 2, "When Our Family Gets Money," is your how-to guide for making a mini-economy system. It shows you how to help your kids build habits of work, sharing, saving, and spending. Part 3, "Tying It All Together," shows you how to avoid missteps and take next steps.

For now, look through the "Think and Teach" questions below. You'll see this section at the end of every chapter. Use it to see where you are with your thinking. There are also suggested questions for the kids, so you can start the conversation with them. When you're ready, move on to chapter 1, "The Mini-Economy Quick-Start Guide." It will outline the first practical steps you can take to getting your kids on track to learn the money habits and values they will take with them the rest of their lives. If you're not so sure about whether you're ready to jump into a whole new household system, this quick-start guide will describe how you can try out a mini-economy for just a couple weeks, sort of like a game. You'll come away with some new lessons and experiences as well as an extra dose of confidence for teaching your kids about money, work, and life.

Let's jump in.

— THINK AND TEACH —

Questions for Parents

1. Do your children get chances to make choices about money? If so, how? If not, what gets in the way?
2. Do your children get chances to make meaningful choices over time? If so, how? If not, what gets in the way?
3. What values does your family have?
4. What are your family's goals?
5. How did you learn about money when you were young?
6. What has led to your current money habits?
7. What good habits do your children have?

Questions for Children

1. What are some things you care about?
2. What is a happy family like?
3. Do you care about money? Why or why not?
4. What is money?
5. What is money used for?
6. What would happen if there was no money?

Lessons for Children

1. We should decide what is important for us in life.
2. We need to take good care of ourselves.

3. We need to take good care of others.
4. A family is like a team. Family members help each other.
5. Money helps us trade. Instead of trading one thing for another, we can get things we want at different times.
6. Money helps us compare how valuable something is.
7. We can use money that we save to buy big things in the future.

1

The Mini-Economy Quick-Start Guide

This chapter is for people who don't want to hear me blah-blah-blah-ing about ideas and just want to get this mini-economy show on the road. I also expect it will cause questions to bubble up in your mind, which I will answer throughout the rest of the book.

If you want to go even faster—as in you don't even want to read this whole chapter!—check out the quick-start templates. I've tried to make it easy for you. You can use these templates as a guide for mini-economy materials, or you can make your own. Just remember that for young kids who can't read yet, it helps to draw pictures on lists, money, and coupons.

You can begin in six (or seven) steps.

1. Decide what items and privileges the money will buy.
2. Design and print the money.
3. Assign jobs to everyone in the family.
4. Make a budget: Share-Save-Spend.
5. Have Store Day.
6. Optional but worth it: Set up businesses.
7. Do it!

Decide What Items and Privileges the Money Will Buy

Before you launch your mini-economy, you need to get buy-in from the kids. First, emphasize that when everybody does chores, it helps make the house nice for everybody. It also makes it so that no one person has to do all the work. Be sure they know their work makes a difference and you value it. It's critical to frame chores in this way before moving on to the tangible rewards they can get. (For more discussion on chores, see chapter 5.)

Next, tell them that instead of just cleaning up after themselves, they will have a chance to buy extra things, have many fun family outings, help people who need help, and make the house an even nicer place to live. (For more discussion on saving and spending, see chapters 7 and 8.)

They'll be doing a mini-economy. They'll have a job or jobs that improve the house for everyone. Also, they'll get paid in money you will design together. You'll set up a store in the house where they can buy things like toys, candy, screen time, adventures, games, and privileges. They'll get a chance to sell things they make in the store. And they'll learn how they can use their work and money to help others.

Make some suggestions about what the store should sell (which you can get from this book). Ask them what sorts of things they'd like to see in the store. Write them down. Let them see you take their suggestions seriously. This builds buy-in. For example, my children like stuffed animals, special outings that include snacks, and screen time (which we usually keep quite limited). If they suggest something that simply won't work or that contradicts your family's values, discuss why that option won't work. You are already building an understanding with them around the mini-economy. But be sure to include some surprises to unveil the first time you do the store.

If you want to teach them about generosity, plan to teach them to set aside money for donating (see chapter 6).

Next, tell them there are some things you will all buy together. The family will vote on a goal to save for—and pay for that goal with taxes. All citizens need to pay taxes, which are money the government (in this case, the parents) collects for things that all the citizens enjoy together. In real life, taxes pay for firefighters, police officers, trash collection, and building and repairing roads. But in this economy, the kids will save up tax payments for a special family purchase or outing. (The best privileges are things they usually wouldn't get or of which they usually get a limited amount.) For example, they could earn a trip to the county fair where parents will buy them food, games, and rides, and Dad wouldn't even constantly tell them "No, that's too expensive!"

Here's how I laid it out to my kids one summer: "We can use taxes to buy something small and cheap, something big and expensive, or something in between."

- Small thing (low taxes): doughnuts at Sugar Shack.
- Medium thing (medium taxes): trip to the movies with popcorn.
- Big thing (high taxes): trip to the county fair with rides and food.

Discuss the options with them—again, you are getting buy-in. Tell them that expensive things will take more tax money, so they would have less to spend at the store. But if they want the tax level to be higher or lower, that is OK as long as they agree. Tell them that citizens get to decide together what the tax level will be. (For more discussion on taxes, see chapter 6.)

Design and Print the Money

Designing money is a fun activity for kids. You can print out a money template from the quick-start templates or draw your own. First, come up with a name for your money. In this book, I'll refer to play money as "Bucks," but you can name yours whatever you want! In our house it's DayBucks. Show them some real money. Point out the designs and writing on it. Explain how money has pictures and words that remind people what their country is about. Ask them what sorts of pictures and words your family money should have.

Next, make money designs in different denominations. It makes sense to follow United States dollars (and many other currencies) in creating ones, fives, tens, and twenties. You can divide up the task of designing the money between different children. Give older children—or the more artistic one—the task of doing the 1-Buck bills, since these are the most common.

You can simply print off lots of money, either in color or in black-and-white. You can have the children color the money, or not. (We allowed our younger children to color the DayBucks, leading to well-designed money with horrendous coloring. No problem.) If you don't have access to a printer, you can buy play money or use some other item in place of money. (See page 26 for suggestions.)

If you have a child who loves to save, you might need to create more money. For example, my now-ten-year-old Calvin is holding a competition with himself to see how much he can save up (his siblings do not share in this fixation). Over time, he's mopped up most of our mini-economy's paper money. We've created more, keeping track of how much extra money we've "minted."

A tip: Make sure to have loads of 1-Buck bills. You will probably need more than you think you will. Many 1-Buck bills sit for a time in the tax cup and the sharing (i.e., donation) cup. This takes them out of circulation, which means you can run low if you are not careful. And it's not fun to constantly make change.

Here's what I recommend. For each person, including adults, print:

- Twenty 1-Buck bills
- Five 5-Buck bills
- Five 10-Buck bills
- Two 20-Buck bills (or more as needed if one of your children hoards money)

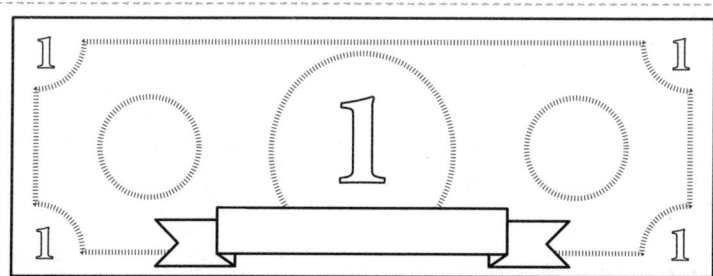

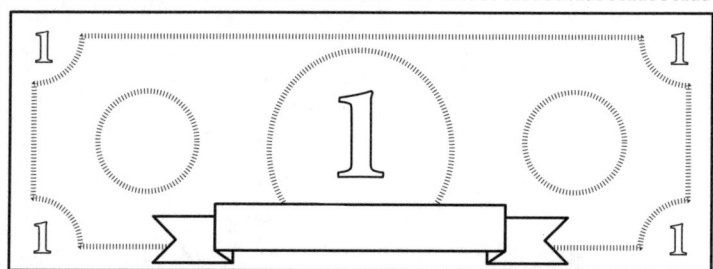

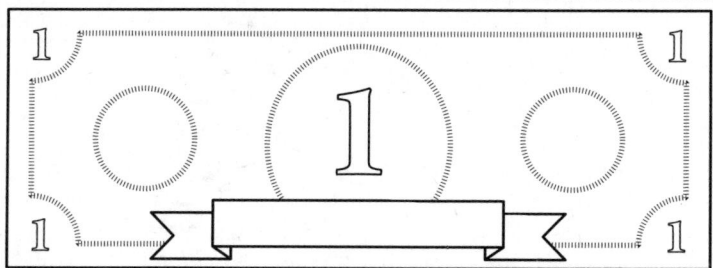

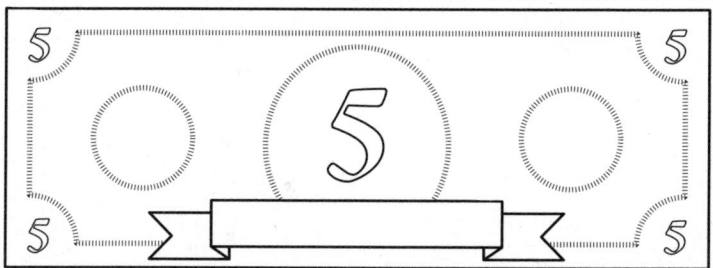

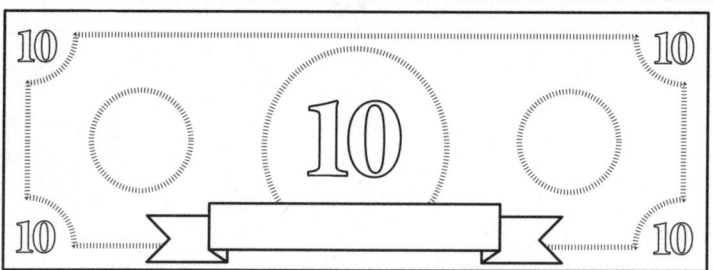

OTHER KINDS OF MONEY

Here are some additional currency options you can use:

- **Real money.** This helps your children learn about the value of real money; there is no need to convert it to play money. The drawback is that it can get expensive, and you can't control the price of the things in your store as much. You also miss an opportunity to teach the children about money, since designing it themselves prompts them to think about what actually makes money valuable.
- **Quarters only.** This gives you a bonus opportunity to teach kids about different parts of your country. You can have them find the states on a map or even make a "map" using quarters.
- **Ledger only.** Rather than giving them currency (cash), just have them keep records of how much money they have. This can be a cleaner process, and it gives you the opportunity to teach that money still has value even when it's just numbers on paper.
- **Anything, really.** Money can be anything that is portable, durable, divisible, scarce, and easily measurable. Have fun and be creative about what you use as money.

Kids may want real money, especially if they are older. We allow this by making DayBucks exchangeable for US dollars. Our exchange rate is 2 DayBucks = 1 dollar. This anchors the mini-economy to the real economy and makes the kids always willing to earn money. Remember, you can use the family store to make some items relatively cheaper than they would be at a real store, and others more expensive.

Assign Jobs to Everyone in the Family

Both kids and parents get jobs. Create a list of what needs to be done around the house. Ask your children what sorts of tasks they think are necessary, and allow them to choose which jobs they want. You can also allow them to create their own jobs—bearing in mind that their work is supposed to benefit the entire family.

Give each job a title. This adds to the fun and helps communicate about who is doing what. For example, the Zookeeper's job is to put stuffed animals away and to fill the cat's food and water bowls. Preschoolers love the idea of being a Zookeeper.

It's simplest to make each job pay the same salary, though some classroom teachers using a mini-economy have paid different salaries. If kids want more money, they should have the option to do extra jobs.

Here is a list of jobs used in household mini-economies. Of course, you can (and should) make up your own as you see fit.

- **Librarian**: picks up and reshelves books, reads bedtime stories to younger siblings, writes a book.
- **Chef's assistant**: wipes off table, sweeps floor, sometimes helps prepare a meal.
- **Zookeeper**: feeds pet, puts pet out and calls it in, picks up stuffed animals.
- **Shoekeeper**: takes shoes out of the car, puts shoes in their places, matches socks. Yes, keeping track of children's shoes is an entire job all by itself.
- **Hospitality worker**: tidies rooms, dusts, greets adult guests nicely and offers them a drink.
- **Equipment manager**: picks up outdoor and sports equipment and puts it away, pumps up balls and bike tires.
- **Gardener**: pulls weeds, plants flowers and vegetables, waters plants, clips hedges.

- **Musician**: practices and plays a weekly recital for the family, makes playlists for listening in the car, cleans instruments and puts them away, puts music away.
- **Bedmaker**: makes beds, folds clean sheets.
- **Ruler of the toys**: organizes toys.
- **Pool attendant**: puts away swimming gear after family returns from pool, hangs up towels, hangs up swimsuits, takes uneaten snacks out of pool bag, hangs up floaties, and organizes swim bags.
- **Trash collector**: empties bathroom trash, takes trash to alley, replaces trash bags.
- **Server**: sets table, fills cups, clears table, loads dishwasher.
- **Dishwasher**: loads dishwasher, dries dishes and puts them away.
- **Laundry attendant**: starts laundry, helps fold clothes.
- **Vehicle technician**: pumps up bike tires, puts vehicles in proper places, maintains vehicles in working order.
- **Accountant**: helps younger sibling count, organize, and budget money.

Jobs should include a skill a child can learn and perhaps a tool a child can use. These build a sense of competence, interest, and pride. (I'll discuss the importance of these more in chapters 2 and 3.)

You can get started with jobs immediately. But you should prepare to have the kids create businesses in which they sell things in the store. This last step (discussed in chapter 9) is what makes this system a true economy in which money flows circularly through the house and in which everyone is both a producer and a consumer—just like in real life.

Note: If you have only one elementary-age child, it's wise to get them started making a business sooner rather than later. That gets the parents involved in the economy, so you have more people

 **Librarian**

 **Chef's Assistant**

 **Equipment Manager**

 **Shoe-keeper**

 **Gardener**

Trash Collector

 **Laundry Attendant**

 **Musician**

 **Ruler of the Toys**

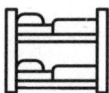 **Bedmaker**

 **Zookeeper**

 **Pool Attendant**

 **Dishwasher**

 **Accountant**

 **Vehicle Technician**

 **Server**

 **Hospitality Worker**

participating instead of just one. You might also consider doing a mini-economy in partnership with another family.

Make a Budget: Share-Save-Spend

Determine how often you want to pay them, and how much. In our summer mini-economy, the kids do their chores three times a week and earn 3 DayBucks each time. They get a 1-DayBuck bonus on payday, Saturday, for having done all their chores that week. This brings it to 10 DayBucks for the week, which makes the math easy. (During the school year they only do jobs once per week and get paid less.)

Before the children spend their newly earned money, they need a plan for it. A money plan is another way of saying a *budget*, though I hesitate to use the word because it freaks people out. Most of us don't budget as well as we'd like. But that's even more of a reason to get your kids used to planning how they give, save, and spend. If they learn at an early age that money needs a plan, they'll be more likely to continue the habit as young adults. I'll discuss budgeting further in chapters 6 and 7. But for the moment, here are some basic pointers on how to get your kids started with a money plan.

I follow the popular Save-Spend-Share method, with a twist: Sharing (or giving or donating) comes first. Sharing can mean giving to charity, nonprofits, or places of worship, or even giving birthday presents to friends. Exactly how you choose to share will differ from family to family. It provides an opportunity to teach kids about community and generosity. Sharing before saving or spending communicates its importance and ensures that it actually happens.

How much money should kids donate? A good place to start is 10 percent, but you can adjust this to suit your family. Find an appropriate place to store the money they donate. You can have the kids decorate whatever container or envelope you use (or make it part of a job). When you've collected a certain amount of Bucks from them, make a real-life donation to whatever organization you've targeted for giving.

Next, the kids should decide how much money they will save. There are two different ways to do this:

1. *Save a certain percentage.* This should be a large proportion of their income, at least 25–50 percent. I recommend this plan if your kids are unlikely to be able to keep themselves from burning up all their income at the family store.

2. *Save whatever amount will get them to their spending goal.* If your kids are genuinely motivated to save up for a bigger ticket item (say, a toy from the family store), they will likely be happy to save the majority of their income, even up to 100 percent. What matters is whether they have a plan. (Talk to them about this using the questions at the end of this chapter and chapter 7. You can also use the included quick-start template.)

Though the second method—saving whatever gets them closer to their goal—may seem helter-skelter and consumption-based, I actually think this way is better. Remember, saving is really just deferred spending. When kids are saving toward a goal, it makes their saving more personal and meaningful. And it makes the trade-off between spending now versus spending later a stark reality.

As with everything in a mini-economy, you know your family best. Decide whether there is a certain percentage kids will be required to save or if they should choose whether to save toward a goal versus spending now.

Have Store Day

This is the moment the kids have been waiting for: the store. Stock the store with homemade coupons for fun events, little treats, and

Saving Plan

Whose? _____

Draw your goal: ✏️

Today's Savings	Total Savings

Draw your 2nd choice
– what you give up ✏️

Work to be done:

higher value items. You should show the kids some or all of the items available in the store before they do their jobs. They need motivation! Furthermore, knowing what is in the store allows them to set goals for their work.

The main thing to remember when deciding what to put in the store is that kids should be able to buy *treats*—that is, things they would not normally get. You don't want to make them buy things they were already getting for free. They should feel that the jobs they are doing are bringing them a benefit. What you do or don't sell in the store can be a delicate choice. (You can read more about what to do and what to avoid in chapter 8.)

Below is a list of things parents have allowed their children to purchase in their stores. But first, here's a disclaimer: Don't judge! There are some things on this list that might make you think, *I wouldn't allow my child to do that*, or *Someone makes their children pay to do* that? Every mini-economy is different, and you can put whatever things in the store you are comfortable with.

Goods
- Candy
- Sugary drinks
- Toys
- Decorations for their rooms
- Stuffed animals
- Clothing items
- Concession-stand items at pool or outing
- Art supplies
- Books
- Coloring books
- Board games or card games
- Sports items: balls, water bottles, and so on
- Things you find at the thrift store or dollar store

Coupons for Services/Experiences

- Outing to museum, sports event, movie theater, and so on
- Sleepover
- Bring a friend on a family outing
- Stay up late
- Extra screen time
- Campfire in backyard
- Sleep in tent in backyard
- Pick something for dinner this week
- Extra dessert
- Keep blanket fort up an extra day (this coupon solved a real-life problem in the Day household)

Remember, you can invite another family to participate in your store. More people in the economy means more fun and enhanced conversations about money. This is especially fun and educational if the other family has a mini-economy too or your kids have their own businesses.

Optional but Worth It: Set Up Businesses

Our family did a mini-economy for several summers before the kids set up businesses. But when we finally did, it was so worth it.

To do this, tell the kids they have the opportunity to earn even more money by starting a business. This business must sell something other people in the family want (either an item or a service). They should also sell something they can provide with a skill they have. That's what running a business is about: what consumers want and what producers can make.

They will sell their product on Store Day. They can sell coupons for services, like making coffee for their parents, or sell items directly, like artwork, cookies, or homemade toys.

35

Mini-Economy

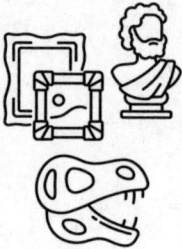

$_____

**Museum
Coupon**

Mini-Economy

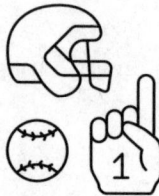

$_____

**Sports Event
Coupon**

Mini-Economy

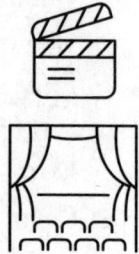

$_____

**Theater
Coupon**

Mini-Economy

$_____

**Sleepover
Coupon**

Mini-Economy

$_____

**Bring a Friend
Coupon**

Mini-Economy

$_____

**Backyard
Tent Camping
Coupon**

Mini-Economy

$____

**Campfire
Coupon**

Mini-Economy

$____

**Sweet Treat
Coupon**

Mini-Economy

T V

$____

**Screen Time
Coupon**

Mini-Economy

$____

**Stay Up Late
Coupon**

Mini-Economy

$____

**Adventure
with Parent
Coupon**

Mini-Economy

$____

_____
Coupon

MINI-ECONOMY 14-DAY CHALLENGE

If you want to dip your toe into a mini-economy, try it out for just a couple weeks by following this quick-start guide. It's a great way to pass time in the summer.

Here are a few tips:

- Make a big deal out of designing and coloring the money. It's a fun project.

- Get the kids on board with a giving and a saving goal. You'll plan to make a donation to a good cause, and the kids will work to get something fun.

- Teach them a new skill for a new job. This should probably involve teaching them how to use a tool. Cleaning up should only be a part of the job.

- The kids should have their own businesses. Brainstorm with them what they should sell.

- Hold at least two Store Days. For the second Store Day, invite some of their friends over and give them mini-economy money to spend. (If you want to be really clever, ask their parents to make them do a job to get the money.) The friends can shop at your kids' businesses as well as the household store.

See? That wasn't so hard. A mini-economy works as a short summer project or as an on-going family organization system. It's flexible. Do what works for you.

Explain to them that they get to choose what price to charge. It should be low enough that people want to pay it but high enough that it is worth their time spent doing the extra work. This is a time for the kids to exercise new freedom and autonomy—they are the bosses now! Making business choices helps them understand how money works in new and surprising ways.

Their business can really thrive if your family invites another family to Store Day. The economy grows, and there are more choices for everyone to make and more lessons to learn. (Read chapter 8 for more details on how to run the store and chapter 9 for a discussion on making a business.)

Do It!

Take the leap! A mini-economy is easy to start and very flexible. It can be extremely simple, extremely complex, or something in between—whatever your family is comfortable with. It is important to start small, then add things as you get more confident. You'll discover new things along the way too. As mini-economy parent Taylor said, "It was a great exercise for our family. I found that we learned so much about our kids' personalities."

As we've talked about, at its most basic form, it must include jobs, money, and a store. It's different from just paying kids for chores, because of the household money system and store. The household money and store allow you a little more control over your kids' experience. In this sense, mini-economy is a teaching tool. It gives you a platform to teach them about life and money values. Seeing how money flows through the mini-economy helps them understand the real world.

■ ■ ■ ■

To recap, here's how to get started: Decide what the kids will be able to buy. Tell them about the new system. Design the currency with them. Assign jobs to all family members. Help kids with their money plan (Share-Save-Spend). Do the store. And make adjustments as you go.

For very small children and very basic mini-economies, you can simplify budgeting and spending to "Save or Spend Day." This is where you give kids the choice between buying something small today or waiting a week to buy something better. That's something that even a three-year-old can understand, and it's also not too intimidating of a system to set up. As kids get closer to middle school age, you'll need to modify the mini-economy to give them more opportunities to use real money. (I discuss this in chapter 12.)

You can add complexity from here. Throughout this book are ideas for extra bells and whistles you can add. A mini-economy is like the board game Othello: It takes a minute to learn but a lifetime to master. There are so many possibilities. Again, it's best to start easy, then grow from there.

Be sure to revisit the later chapters in this book as you get experience and as new questions and ideas start to percolate in your mind. A mini-economy offers endless possibilities. So go for it!

—— THINK and TEACH ——

Questions for Parents

1. Why are you reading this book?
2. How have you managed your kids' money and chores in the past? Have you thought about changing what you do?
3. What about a mini-economy leaves you unconvinced?
4. What about it do you find most interesting?

Questions for Children

1. How do you get the things you want? Does it work?
2. Are there jobs around the house that you do?
3. Have you ever had money? How did you spend it?
4. What if everyone had the same job at home? What if everyone in our city had the same job? Why wouldn't that work?

Lessons for Children

1. To have a nice home, we all need to work together.
2. Some people have different jobs.
3. In real life, people need to produce things to get money, and they need money if they want to buy things.
4. If people work more, they can produce more goods or services. That means there are more things available to buy.

PART 1

WHY WE ARE DOING THIS

Kids don't get enough practice with money. Even if families talk about money together and parents find ways to model good habits, kids still need hands-on experience. Think of all the practice they get learning to read, playing a sport, or creating art projects. By contrast, spending a weekly allowance at the store isn't enough practice with money. Besides, simply spending on candy or something similar doesn't teach them much about how money works in the economy. Kids need dense, age-appropriate, fun experiences about learning how money works.

Here are two reasons kids don't get enough practice.

1. *Parents are uncomfortable with their own financial knowledge and habits*. Often parents don't feel they know enough about money or how to manage it. Sometimes their own financial habits aren't that great. Perhaps money is seen as a very private thing in the family. And sometimes

they just don't know how to communicate these concepts in an age-appropriate way.

2. *Parents and kids lack a context for making meaningful choices about money together.* Parents earn far more money than children. Children find it hard to understand how parents can earn thousands of dollars a year and still insist that the family doesn't have enough money for this or that. For kids, who only handle small amounts of money, it's confusing.

A mini-economy can fix these problems. First, the play money setting is low stakes. Parents can talk with their kids about how to spend play money, even if they're less sure about their own real money habits and knowledge. In a mini-economy, the conversation can flow more easily. Second, parents and kids get to interact with similar amounts of play money that buy real things. The problem of scale goes away.

Last, it gives kids lots of opportunities to practice what to do with money—both as producers and consumers. Research suggests that the elementary school years (ages five to ten) are when kids should be building money habits and norms.[1] Building good habits helps people make better choices over time. This helps us get the things we truly want in the long term. Frittering away money in the short term gets in the way of what people actually want. If kids not only learn but *practice* solid financial habits in the elementary years, they are better positioned to sustain them over a lifetime.[2]

This is the age when kids learn that money needs a plan according to the family's values: Some money is set aside for giving and

1. Consumer Financial Protection Bureau (CFPB), "Building Blocks to Help Youth Achieve Financial Capability: A New Model and Recommendations," pdf, September 2016, https://files.consumerfinance.gov/f/documents/092016_cfpb _BuildingBlocksReport_ModelAndRecommendations_web.pdf.

2. CFPB, "Financial Well-Being: The Goal of Financial Education," pdf, January 2015, https://files.consumerfinance.gov/f/201501_cfpb_report_financial -well-being.pdf.

sharing. Some money is saved for future goals. Some money can be spent now for small treats. And, perhaps most importantly of all, they learn the things people want to buy don't just come from Mom or Dad! They come from work.

As you start to teach your kids about money, you might think of questions like these:

What should kids be learning?

When should they be learning it?

Is it really appropriate to pay kids to do chores, even if it's play money?

Isn't paying kids to do things a form of control that should be discouraged?

Won't paying children for chores take away their motivation to help the family?

What if a child won't do their job?

These are all excellent questions, which I'll seek to answer in chapters 2–4 using research findings.

There certainly are wrong ways to do a mini-economy. Those ways tend to overemphasize rule following and behavior management and underemphasize making choices about money over time. When you've read these chapters, you should have a vision for what you're teaching your children.

There are many practical takeaways for making your mini-economy in part 1. However, it is most useful for parents who are seeking a deeper understanding about teaching kids about money and work. For the extended mini-economy how-to guide, skip to part 2.

45

2

What Kids Should Learn

"I just think that I'll be in debt for the rest of my life, so I might as well make the most of it."

I was standing on the sidewalk talking with my neighbor, a soft-spoken twentysomething who rented the house next to us. She had just told me her good news: She'd been accepted to a master's degree program in creative writing. I congratulated her and was just getting ready to ask her what she liked to write about. But before I could, she mentioned that she didn't know exactly how she'd pay for it, given that she still had lots of student debt from her undergraduate degree.

"Wow, what do you think you're going to do?" I asked, trying to keep the alarm out of my voice. That's when she told me that she didn't expect to ever get out of debt, but she hoped to at least get a good experience from her master's program. It would be something she could look back on with fondness, I suppose, for the rest of her debt-burdened years.

I was struck by the sense of powerlessness in her words and how little faith she had in her future prospects. Learning new skills, as one does with a college degree, is supposed to bring with it new possibilities. For her, it was the opposite.

Our Choices Are Powerful

What was striking about this conversation was my neighbor's *beliefs* about the control, or lack of it, she had over her financial future. She saw herself as a passive object floating down the stream of life, with no strength to change her course. What happened to her was just that: something that happened to her. She moved away not long after that, so I don't know how her story is going. I hope she eventually learned the lesson of Dr. Seuss's classic book *Oh, the Places You'll Go!*: "**You'll** start happening too!"[1]

To be sure, life happens to us. It happens and happens and then happens some more. It's usually not fair. Many people lack complete access to financial services and other parts of the economy. People face discrimination. People's family and community backgrounds can either empower them or disadvantage them, or a mix of both. Relationships can be an asset or a burden. But as the saying goes, something might not be your fault, but it's still your problem. We want our children to grow up with the tools to operate inside their environment and even to change it, not to be ruled by it.

In the realm of money, this is called *financial capability*. The Consumer Financial Protection Bureau (CFPB), a department of the US government, defines financial capability as "the capacity, based on knowledge, skills, and access, to manage financial resources effectively."[2] It's the mental tools that people need to master their finances.

What are the ingredients of financial capability? According to the CFPB, they are:

- Impulse control and the ability to delay gratification in service of future rewards.
- Perseverance in the face of obstacles.

1. Dr. Seuss, *Oh, the Places You'll Go!* (Random House, 1990), 9. Emphasis added.
2. CFPB, "Building Blocks to Help Youth."

- Belief in their ability to manage money and achieve financial goals.
- A tendency to make financial decisions in light of their own standards rather than in comparison to other people.[3]

We can summarize these ingredients as "the ability to *work* toward financial *goals* that are based on your *values*." Let's go through these terms one by one.

Work

Kids are used to doing schoolwork. But they are not used to working for money or connecting money to financial goals. Doing chores for money is one way to teach them to work to pursue financial goals that are based on their values. (There is a lively debate about whether kids should be paid to do chores. See chapter 4.)

Research shows that families suffer from a lack of vision and goals when it comes to getting kids to do chores. Consider this scenario recorded in *Fast-Forward Family*. This is a real-life conversation in which a father and mother are trying to get their child to stop playing a board game with Mom and do some work:

Father: Let's not play [now]. Son, come here, (you're) gonna help me out with the dishes. Come on.
Brian: No:::
Father: Yes. Now. C'mon. Then you play. Let's go.
Brian: No uhhh ((*sniffs and tears up*)). . . . Why do *I* gotta do the dishes? ((*crying*))
Father: We'll do it together.
Brian: No:::
Father: You can either put it in the sink . . . or you can rinse it . . . or you can pass it to me, you can choose any job you want. . . .

3. CFPB, "Building Blocks to Help Youth."

Brian: Me and Mom play checkers. That's a job.

Father: That's not a job, that's a— that's playing!

Brian: I'm *not* gonna *do* it. . . .

Mother: It would help *me* out.

Father: Don't you want to help Ma? She *cooked*.

The researchers conclude: "[The] father ends up extracting a promise from [the son] that he will help 'next time' and allows him to continue playing the game with his mother."[4]

If that scenario made you cringe, wait until you read the one where parents try to get the kids to work when they're watching TV!

Parents often don't ask kids for help with chores until the parents are tired and flustered. To the children, sudden requests (demands!) that they get up and work feel like arbitrary punishments. It seems to them that if parents are feeling nice, the kids can just play or watch TV. But if the parents are feeling mean, then the kids have to clean something up or do homework.

Chores can be unpleasant, and kids often will not want to do them. Parents often respond by being too strict and arbitrary or by attempting to set up motivational systems that backfire. Eventually they just give up. But with the help of an easy-to-understand mini-economy, parents have a sustainable system for doing chores and can help kids learn how work fits together with money and with reaching their goals.

Goals

When I say "goals," I mean *all* the goals: big important ones as well as little shallow ones. All of them require people to make choices after considering the trade-offs. Even small children can do that.

4. Wendy Klein and Marjorie Harness Goodwin, "Chores," in *Fast-Forward Family: Home, Work, and Relationships in Middle-Class America*, ed. Eleanor Ochs and Tamar Kremer-Sadlik (University of California Press, 2013), 117–18.

Try this: Make a list of around six goals you might pursue in a given day. Here's an example:

1. Go to the coffee shop at 1:30 for after-lunch coffee.
2. Open a new 529 account to begin saving money for the kids' college fund.
3. Meet your work project deadline.
4. Check in on your friend you haven't heard from in a while.
5. Work on your next assignment in your master's degree program.
6. Get the car's oil changed.

Now, say the day is so busy that you can only reach four of these goals. Which two would you cut out? It's a tough choice, even when these aren't real choices! We all feel the pinch of what economists call *scarcity*, which is when we don't have the resources we need to fulfill all of our goals. Most of the time, the scarce resource is *us*. There isn't enough of us to do everything we want to do!

Think about the choices you might make on a normal day:

- Should I go into work early so I don't fall behind on my project?
- Should I go out to lunch or bring my lunch?
- Should I start this uncomfortable but necessary conversation with a family member?
- Should we sign the kids up for travel soccer?
- Should we get a membership to the science museum?
- Should I give money to the animal shelter?
- Should I give money to the panhandler on the sidewalk? (And how should I explain my decision to the kids?)

- Should I save for retirement, college, rainy day fund . . . or do I even have enough money to do those things?

Think about the choices a kid might face:

- If another kid is breaking the rules of the game, should I lash out? Or should I just let them do it?
- Should I come to the dinner table when I'm called? Or should I just play a little longer?
- Should I spend all my money on things now? Or should I save for later?

Children are clearly more impulsive than adults and aren't as likely to make choices in a rational, considered way. But part of learning to manage resources is to grow in being goal oriented.

Having goals isn't enough, because we can have goals and still not know exactly what to do about them. We still need to choose which goals to pursue first and how much effort to put into them. That is, we need to learn to prioritize. How do we do that? We put our goals in order of importance based on our values. Then we can work toward our goals in a purposeful way. Kids need goal-oriented practice with money. That's what it means to teach a kid to save.

Values

Prioritization isn't just about whether or not you are "good with money" or even whether you're goal oriented. At the root, it's about your values. What do you think is important? Are there some things that are just the right thing (or the wrong thing) to do, regardless of their impact on your life? Are your money habits going to help you reach your goals? Are there some values you hold so deeply that you barely notice them (like, for example, the need for safety)?

First come values. Then comes the economy. Your family's choices in the economy reflect your family's values.

In *Values-Based Parenting*, Andy Yarborough explains values like this: "What you seek first organizes the rest of your life."[5] In other words, the goal you set as your number one priority will affect all your other lesser (but still important) goals. Many of us can't explain or define our values. But defining our values is critical because it allows us to understand why we prioritize the goals that we do.

A person's or a family's values are very personal. But people often share similar values, usually within the boundaries of culture, religion, region, or other group. I'm not going to tell you what goals you *should* have. Your family should think and talk about your values, where they come from, why they are important, and how to pursue them.

A mini-economy is a way to teach kids about money. But parents are not just teaching facts about money. They are teaching how the family ought to think about money. In order to do so well, parents need a vision for what they want their children to know. This is where values come in.

Here are some categories of money values parents often want their children to learn about:

1. Stewardship
2. Generosity
3. Self-control
4. Justice
5. Work and rest

How do these values show themselves in a mini-economy? I'll use our household mini-economy as an example. As you read this list,

5. Andy Yarborough, *Values-Based Parenting: Parenting Well in a Culture of Chaos*, Kindle ed. (self-published, 2024), 9.

think about what values you hold that affect your economic life and what you want to pass on to your children.

- *Stewardship*. This means using what we have well. It means that we have a responsibility to use our resources not just for our own pleasure.
- *Generosity*. Our children have to donate (share) a tenth of their income before they save or spend. This leads to conversations about what that money is used for.
- *Self-control*. This manifests itself as saving. In the family store, kids are faced with the trade-off between getting something small now (spending) or getting something big later (saving).
- *Justice*. Justice is what is right and fair. Children often encounter justice in the form of rules. Children may not pay to break house rules. The rules are not for sale. If you imagine the economy as a flowing stream, rules are rocks the stream must flow around. The mini-economy helps kids understand what is for sale and what is not.
- *Work and rest*. On job day, the kids are reminded of the importance of working in order to get money to reach their savings goals. This helps them connect work, income, saving, and spending. But it's also important to set time aside for rest. Our family does not work or buy things on Sundays. This is a day off from working, buying, and selling. It's reserved for rest, going to church, serving others, and experiencing a change of pace. Time that is set aside for rest helps children (and adults) draw healthy boundaries around their work.

Can elementary-age children grow toward financial capability? Of course they can. Your mini-economy will give your children practice managing work and money. While they are doing this, you can explain what is happening by using age-appropriate lessons like these:

- We can't have everything we want. But we can work to get the things that are most important to us.
- Let's make a plan.
- Choosing is refusing. When we choose one thing, we give up something else.
- All our choices have costs and benefits (bad things and good things).
- We can spend money on something small now or save for something big later.
- We buy things with money, and we get money from working.
- Our work helps others.
- We work to make the things we buy and trade with others.
- Money makes trade easier.[6]

If you were to just tell the children lessons like these, it would be difficult for them to understand. But in a mini-economy, they continually encounter situations in which they need new knowledge

---

6. If that list made sense and was helpful to you, then congratulations! You can do economics after all. These things can be and have been taught effectively to children using mini-economies. Many come from classic classroom programs such as Marilyn Kourilsky's Mini-Society and Harlan Day's *The Classroom Mini-Economy*. For examples from education research, see the following studies:

Michael Batty et al., "Experiential Financial Education: A Field Study of 'My Classroom Economy' in Elementary Schools," *Economics of Education Review* 78 (2020): 102014.

Stephen Day and Christine L. Bae, "Developing Authentic Performance Assessments in a Classroom Mini-Economy: Reflections on the Process of Design," in *Design Research in Social Studies Education: Critical Lessons from an Emerging Field*, ed. Beth C. Rubin, Eric B. Freedman, and Jongsung Kim (Routledge, 2019), 84–106.

Marilyn Kourilsky and Jack Hirshleifer, "Mini-Society vs. Token Economy: An Experimental Comparison of the Effects on Learning and Autonomy of Socially Emergent and Imposed Behavior Modification," *Journal of Educational Research* 69, no. 10 (1976): 376–81.

to understand what they're doing. For example, once I asked my two sons (ages seven and nine) what the best way to save a lot of money was: to spend less or earn more? They didn't understand the question, even when I rephrased it. But when I put it like this, they got it: "If you wanted to get more money for your savings goal, would you buy less at the family store or do extra jobs?" They immediately knew what I was talking about, and they both had strong (and opposite) opinions about what to do. It started an argument in the car—the good kind!—about what the best choice would be.

Studies using mini-economy-style classroom programs show many positive results. Some of this research goes back decades and some is new, but all of it points in the same direction: This style of program is an effective and responsible way to teach kids.

- Students who were part of the My Classroom Economy program improved financial literacy more than students who were taught with traditional instruction.[7]
- Students who did the Mini-Society program were more likely to weigh the costs and benefits of their choices than students who weren't using the program.[8]
- In my own studies, I've observed students using math, doing market research, discussing ethics, and debating the most efficient ways to use scarce resources when making mini-economy business decisions.[9]
- I've also observed students making connections between classroom learning and business decisions in the mini-economy. The mini-economy felt relevant to them.[10]

7. Batty et al., "Experiential Financial Education."

8. Marilyn Kourilsky and Edna Graff, "Children's Use of Cost-Benefit Analysis: Developmental or Non-Existent," pdf, July 1985, Education Resources Information Center, https://files.eric.ed.gov/fulltext/ED261948.pdf.

9. Stephen Harlan Day, "How Elementary Teachers Use Classroom Mini-Economies When Guided by the C3 Framework," PhD dissertation (North Carolina State University, 2015).

10. Day and Bae, "Developing Authentic Performance Assessments."

Gaining confidence with money early in life is especially important for girls. Studies consistently show that females are less confident with money than males and show lower levels of financial literacy.[11] But there is evidence that mini-economies can help with this too. One study showed that before doing the Mini-Society program in school, girls tended to say that entrepreneurship was for boys. After doing the program, they said that both boys and girls could be good at business, and results showed no difference between girls' and boys' (positive) risk-taking, persistence, and economic success.[12] This improved view of money was likely due to students' positive experience with risk-taking as they ran classroom businesses and made money choices.

A mini-economy is about giving children access to many experiences with money. This creates teachable moments—a powerful method for helping children learn about money, work, and life.[13]

We live in an increasingly complex world. The world is scary, but it also provides amazing opportunities that confident and savvy young people will take full advantage of. Our choices are powerful. As we will see in the next chapter, it's important for kids to learn early in life that they can be confident and capable money managers. Money will work for them, not against them. They will become confident young adults who *happen* to the world around them. It will be a joy to see what they can do.

---

11. Annamaria Lusardi, Olivia S. Mitchell, and Vilsa Curto, "Financial Literacy Among the Young," *Journal of Consumer Affairs* 44, no. 2 (2010): 358–80; Ani Caroline Grigion Potrich, Kelmara Mendes Vieira, and Guilherme Kirch, "How Well Do Women Do When It Comes to Financial Literacy? Proposition of an Indicator and Analysis of Gender Differences," *Journal of Behavioral and Experimental Finance* 17 (2018): 28–41.

12. Marilyn Kourilsky and Michael Campbell, "Sex Differences in a Simulated Classroom Economy: Children's Beliefs About Entrepreneurship," *Sex Roles* 10 (1984): 53–66.

13. Margaret Sherrard Sherraden et al., "Financial Capability in Children: Effects of Participation in a School-Based Financial Education and Savings Program," *Journal of Family and Economic Issues* 32 (2011): 385–99.

—— THINK and TEACH ——

Questions for Parents

1. Did your parents teach you about money when you were young?
2. What did you learn about money from your family when you were a child? (Often, the lessons we learned weren't explicitly taught but rather picked up along the way.)
3. When you envision a "good financial life," what do you think of?
4. What financial values do you have? How do they (or don't they) overlap with the "good financial life" you thought about in the previous question?
5. What lesson that you learned as a child do you want to pass on to your children? What do you want to teach them that you never learned?
6. Are there any money habits in your family (either in your kids or in you) you'd like to change?
7. How do you and your spouse's money values compare? How are they similar? Different?

Questions for Children

1. When you get money, what do you like to do with it?
2. Do you have money saved?
3. Do you like to save money?
4. What is good about knowing you have money saved?

5. Do you know about any of the choices your parents have to make about money?
6. When you get money, what do you think your parents would like you to do with it?

Lessons for Children

1. I can produce.
2. I can save.
3. I can learn new things.
4. I can trade.
5. I can get better.
6. I should ask questions like:
   - What's the cost?
   - What's the benefit?
   - What opportunities do I give up?
   - What could I do instead?
   - What's my next best choice?

3

When Kids Should Learn

Many kids start getting practice with money too late; they should be learning about money when they are in elementary school. When parents do teach them, what they learn might not be age appropriate. With due respect to enthusiastic parents who regale their kids with disquisitions on compound interest and "fractional reserve banking," this just isn't the time. I know; I'm one of those parents.

Now is the time for kids to learn money habits and values, not too many facts. Your magic words for elementary-age kids are "When our family gets money, we . . ." Demonstrate these habits with your own money, explain why you do it, draw the kids into conversations, and set up systems so they can develop the same habits and values. You can do these practices in normal, everyday life, but you'll have many more opportunities in your mini-economy. And if your own financial habits aren't that good, the mini-economy is a good way to practice and demonstrate some better habits in cooperation with your family.

Stages and Skills

Below is a handy chart from the CFPB summarizing the research and showing what kids should be learning as they grow up.[1] Though each category has an age boundary, children should keep learning each category as they mature. For example, children should be learning self-control when they are toddlers, but self-control is something we must practice our whole lives.

Primary Development Stages for Youth Building Blocks for Financial Capability

	❶ Executive function	❷ Financial habits and norms	❸ Financial knowledge and decision-making skills
	Self-control, working memory, problem-solving	*Healthy money habits, norms, rules of thumb*	*Factual knowledge, research and analysis skills*
Early childhood (ages 3–5)	✔	Early values and norms	Basic numeracy
Middle childhood (ages 6–12)	⌄	✔	Basic money management
Adolescence and young adulthood (ages 13–21)	Development continues	Development continues	✔

Here's how to interpret the chart:

- In early childhood (ages 3–5), children grow in executive function, which is the ability to manage one's thoughts and emotions and therefore one's own behavior. They learn self-control and problem-solving and grow in their working memory. (Working memory is the ability to manage complexity; it's what you use to keep your thoughts

1. CFPB, "Building Blocks to Help Youth."

straight.) All of this helps them manage their own behavior. People continue to develop and grow executive function throughout life.

- In middle childhood (ages 6–12), children develop financial habits and norms and rules of thumb (such as "save before you spend"). These build on other early values and norms learned in the preschool years, like "share" and "use words." This is the category parents most often need help with and that a mini-economy is best for developing.

- Adolescence and young adulthood (ages 13–21) is the time to learn financial knowledge and decision-making skills. Factual knowledge, research, and analysis skills are developed by building on basic numeracy (math) learned in elementary school and basic money management learned (hopefully) at home.[2] We use these skills for money management every day for the rest of our lives!

Look at column 1, "executive function." You can teach this mainly by *being a good parent* in the most basic sense. You know, the things you are initially baffled about as a parent of a preschooler but eventually settle into with experience, some helpful books, and a lot of patience. It's about keeping kids safe and well-fed, teaching them about right and wrong, giving them age-appropriate challenges, teaching about boundaries, involving them in family rhythms, letting them do lots of unstructured play with friends, reading to them, reading to them some more, and many other things. If you're already doing these things, well done! You've already set your child on the path to financial capability. As they grow, their executive function also grows, giving them the crucial

2. Research consistently shows that math skills are linked to financial capability. One doesn't need to be a math whiz to be financially capable, but it's important to encourage kids to have a growth mindset in math. See Annamaria Lusardi, "Numeracy, Financial Literacy, and Financial Decision-Making," *Numeracy* 5, no. 1 (2012): article 2, http://dx.doi.org/10.5038/1936-4660.5.1.2.

adult skills of self-control, thinking about their thinking, setting goals, and managing resources over time.

Column 2, "financial habits and norms," is when children want to know what "we" as a family do—and it's time to teach them. Whenever you give children opportunities to manage resources, work toward goals, or make meaningful choices over time, you're helping them in this area. But they should also start attaching those habits to money and work.

The CFPB report explains:

> Financial socialization occurs through implicit observation and through direct instruction. Parents of elementary schoolers can model healthy choices, behaviors, and attitudes as they engage in day-to-day and monthly activities, such as paying bills or grocery shopping. Children observe these actions and implicitly draw conclusions and internalize financial behaviors and norms—for example, always taking a shopping list to the grocery store. Parents also provide explicit, direct financial lessons when they set standards and expectations. . . .
>
> During this developmental stage, children usually begin to grasp abstract concepts that underpin personal finance, such as managing a household budget. In middle childhood, youth are more fully able to understand the future and can determine the timing of things happening months away.[3]

Of course, I would add that the elementary years are when kids need many opportunities to practice using money. The mini-economy gives a holistic and robust way to teach these skills and habits so kids can be fully ready to embrace more complex knowledge when they become teenagers.

Column 3, "financial knowledge and decision-making skills," is when kids are growing toward financial maturity and can benefit

---

3. CFPB, "Building Blocks to Help Youth," 22–23. For ideas about what to do at the grocery store, see my articles on Substack at *Paper Robots: Helping Families Talk About Money and Work* such as "Prices Are Clues" and "How to Stop Your Kids from Bugging You to Buy Stuff," www.drstephenday.com.

from lessons on financial concepts like budgeting, compound interest, credit, and risk. In fact, they really should learn about these things, because their choices bring adult consequences, as so many choices that teenagers make do. Eighteen-year-olds have the opportunity to set a path for their education and career and also to take on large amounts of debt through credit cards and student loans. They need to get a realistic picture of what they can handle.

When we bring children up in a stable environment and instill solid family financial habits, as they mature they become ready to soak up the financial knowledge adults need. (In chapter 12, I'll discuss kids' transition out of the mini-economy and into teenage work—and on into post–high school work and education.) Take heart that with a solid foundation of experience with money and work in your mini-economy, kids will learn about adult finances quickly, and the lessons will stick.

What to Do

Children need to pratice making meaningful choices about money over time. As a parent, you should provide structure and guidance so they can encounter such choices and grow in their ability to manage them.

I'll write it again: **Children need to practice making meaningful choices about money over time.** Let's break that sentence down part by part.

Children. Again, people are never too young to start learning about work, money, resources, and the things they buy. Some of the things we teach our children come naturally to many parents, especially our desire to protect, nurture, and teach them, as well as our desire to set clear boundaries and expectations—to have family rules that are clearly, consistently, and caringly enforced. If you're doing these things, you've already given them the start they need. Good job! You're on track.

Meaningful. By this word, I mean two things. First, what kids learn about money is based on their family's values. For example, "saving money" is a great money habit, but why are we saving? There could be any number of reasons: to gain financial security, to buy lavish things, to avoid being greedy for immediate gratification, to sustain a certain lifestyle, to avoid poverty, to have enough to share with others, to avoid being a burden to others, or something else. (Think: Which of these reasons is most motivating for you?) Second, the choices kids face should be real choices, not choices that have only one good answer. I mean *hard* choices, such as "I am dying for candy now, but I really want to save up to buy that skateboard," or "I really want to play, but if I do an extra job instead I can save up for that skateboard faster." These choices don't necessarily have a correct answer. That's entirely the point. In a mini-economy, your children get the chance to consider the trade-offs and stride confidently into their decisions. That's a habit that will serve them well as they grow up.

Choices. A healthy financial life begins with self-control and problem-solving, then moves on to a basic understanding of values and norms about managing money. How can children practice these things if they don't have an opportunity to make meaningful choices? And how can they make meaningful choices about money if they don't have their own money to spend? Of course, parents could just give children money to spend on things they want. But what about *meaning* and *values*? If kids get money without making any effort, what does that teach them? And if they only get money for treats but don't have the opportunity to choose whether to save or spend, what lesson do they learn? A mini-economy gives children a robust environment in which they can make meaningful choices. When children consistently get to make meaningful choices within a safe, coherent framework, they build autonomy and confidence.

Furthermore, many choices we may give kids are more like non-choices. For example, "Obey or else." In fact, this applies to pretty much any choice for which one option is "Or else!" Such a choice-making environment is so circumscribed that it leaves children constantly looking to a parent, teacher, or some other authority figure for what to do. Don't misunderstand me: I'm not saying there shouldn't be rules. There definitely should be. In fact, this book will help you think about when to give kids a rules-based choice ("You made this mess, so you have to clean it up") versus an economic choice that helps them learn to manage resources ("Your job is to clean up the mess in the playroom, so you'll need to do that if you want to get closer to your saving goal.")

About money. Ultimately you want to teach your children about the time, effort, persistence, and creativity of production (work): the products that we buy, the trades we make, and the goals that we pursue. But we represent these things with money. Money allows us to communicate about how valuable something is, to save up to buy things, and to make trading easier. But money can be a mystery to children (and adults). A mini-economy allows kids to learn important lessons about work, production, trade, saving, giving, spending, sharing, and more in a somewhat controlled though still authentic environment. It provides a platform to introduce children to economic life. Money ties together all the myriad choices in our economic lives and allows us to communicate about them, make plans for them, and to trade with each other. It makes the complex world of production and consumption simple enough for us to understand.

A mini-economy uses play money. Why? Play money allows a family to set up an economy that is largely contained inside the house. The money circulates among family members rather than going straight out the door to a real-life store. With play money, kids can see how money moves through the economy. A play-money economy gives kids the opportunity for lots of practice with financial choices. With real money and a traditional allowance, kids are usually faced with the two-dimensional choice to save (for a toy) or spend (for candy). In a play-money economy, the kids face multidimensional choices in which they give, save, spend, vote on taxes, build businesses, make deals, and take part in any number of creative additions to your economy that you choose. Children learn not only how to manage money but also about how it flows.

Over time. Being able to delay gratification, make plans, and execute plans over a period of time is a sophisticated undertaking. It's this sort of long-run thinking that will aid children throughout life in whatever they are doing. This includes staying out of trouble, getting an education, saving for retirement, and using their time wisely. One mistake parents sometimes make when giving their children a money choice is not adding in a time factor. If the decision only concerns the here and now, it cuts out an important part of most difficult decisions. A real economy is all about the importance of time: time we spend working, time we spend waiting while we save, and time during which we delay gratification. When kids make meaningful choices over time, they learn that the best things in life are worth waiting for, planning for, and staying consistent and faithful for.

Of course, those "best things" are not products bought in a market. They are the big goals that align with our fundamental values. These are often relationships, principles, beliefs, and other intangible things. They are also things that require delaying gratification in order to enjoy them to their fullest. When kids learn to extend their time horizon to be able to "see" the good things that lie in the future, they've developed a skill that will help them for the rest of their lives.

—— THINK AND TEACH ——

Questions for Parents

1. At what age should children start learning about money?
2. How can you involve your children in family financial decisions?
3. What are the benefits of using a mini-economy to teach financial skills?
4. How can you model healthy financial choices and behaviors for your children?
5. What are the key financial habits and norms children should learn in middle childhood?
6. How can you help your children understand the connection between work and money?

Questions for Children

1. What do you think our family does when we get money?
2. What is one reason to save money before spending it?
3. What are some ways you can earn money in our mini-economy?
4. Do you remember a time when you had to choose to wait for something?
5. Do you remember a time when you chose not to wait for something?
6. What are two good reasons we might want to wait for something? Isn't it better to get everything we want now?

7. Is there a time when a choice you made didn't work out like you thought it would?

Lessons for Children

1. We need to practice how we use money.
2. We work to get money.
3. Everyone has to wait to get things they want, even grown-ups. ("Here's a time I had to wait . . .")
4. We can choose to get small things now or big things later.
5. Sometimes the first thing we feel like doing isn't the best idea.
6. How we use our money matters.
7. We make the best plans we can, but sometimes things don't work out like we thought they would.

4

Should Kids Be Paid to Do Chores?

A mini-economy is not a behavior control system. It is a teaching system. Kids don't get paid for following the rules, and they shouldn't. The rules aren't for sale.

But they do get paid for doing their jobs. Should they? Many parents and parenting gurus say no. In fact, pretty much any media or book I've seen about kids and personal finance puts this issue front and center, and there's a lot of disagreement. I don't want to simply repeat this conversation, but I will offer some perspective from research on psychological needs and motivation. I hope this will help you teach your children how to make meaningful choices about money and work over time.

Here's some objections to paying kids for chores:

- "They shouldn't get paid for picking up their own mess!"
- "If I start paying them for chores, then they won't do any work unless they're paid!"
- "They have to do chores because they live here."

If I am reading these critiques correctly, they seem concerned with both *motivation* and *values*. That is, children should learn to do chores because working for the family is the right thing to do.

I am sympathetic to these concerns, but I think there are still reasons to pay the children for some tasks. For starters, the stakes in the Great Allowance Debate aren't as high as some of us think. We don't have to choose one side or the other because we can simply pay children for some jobs but not others.

Here is what I recommend. I'll explain why in a minute.

- Kids should clean up their own messes without getting paid.
- Many parents set up systems in which kids are not paid for doing their basic chores but do get paid for "extra jobs." I support this system, and it lines up with research results.
- I recommend dividing chores into three categories: family work, service work, and mini-economy jobs. Kids only get paid for mini-economy jobs. This allows family rules to remain intact ("You do this work because you're part of the family") while motivating kids to do extra work, improve their skills, and make meaningful choices about money.

Parents who pay for chores need to understand that payment is not a replacement for family values. But if kids only do family work and never get paid for jobs, they don't learn the connection between work and money. They don't get the opportunity to practice making meaningful choices about work over time.

Self-Determination Theory

To discuss the connection between work and money, I use self-determination theory, a very useful psychological theory that seeks to describe what leads to mental well-being and motivation.[1] Self-determination theory posits that all people (in every place and every time) are motivated and find well-being when they are supported in three key areas:

- *Autonomy.* This means "value-aligned-ness"; that is, how much something lines up with what you believe to be true and important. It does *not* mean isolation.
- *Competence.* Success feels good. If you can feel the "flow" of expertise or growth in some activity, you'll want to do it more. It is related to having a growth mindset, which means you don't think your abilities are fixed; you can work to improve them.
- *Relatedness.* This refers to how connected you feel to others when you're doing a task. Knowing that your activity supports a community—and the community supports you—motivates you.[2] It's a sense of belonging.

It is helpful to think of these three pillars of well-being and motivation when parenting in any situation, including when teaching about money and work. Parenting that supports a child's growth in autonomy, competence, and relatedness helps the child grow more confident, secure, engaged, curious, active, and self-regulated. But this takes time. Lots of time. A whole childhood, really. Supporting autonomy isn't an in-the-moment tactic to get a kid who doesn't want to do something to suddenly want to do it. It's a way to bring them up so they learn to value things that are valuable and to act accordingly.

1. Richard M. Ryan and Edward L. Deci, "Intrinsic and Extrinsic Motivation from a Self-Determination Theory Perspective: Definitions, Theory, Practices, and Future Directions," *Contemporary Educational Psychology* 61 (2020): 101860.
2. A related but different framework that I find helpful is the "RBG Framework." "RBG" stands for relevance, belonging, and growth mindset. For more discussion, see my article "How Do I Motivate Kids?," *Paper Robots*, June 4, 2024, www.drstephenday.com/p/how-do-i-motivate-the-kids-to-do.

When I first read about this theory, it seemed overconfident to me. How could these psychologists really say what is best for everyone everywhere, no matter who they are or what they believe? But think of it like this: The theory simply describes any person who is learning to contribute to their own success and that of the people around them, however defined. I think this safely describes a successful person in any context and speaks to any culture or belief system.

When people feel supported in their autonomy, competence, and relatedness, they are more motivated to do things. When people find a task enjoyable and do it for its own sake, they are *intrinsically motivated* to do the task. Something is likely to be intrinsically motivating when it lines up with what self-determination theory calls "basic psychological needs." When they find a task uninteresting or unpleasant, they may still do it if they are *extrinsically motivated.*[3]

Of course, if someone is intrinsically motivated, you don't need to convince them to do something—they are likely doing it already! What parents are concerned about are things that are less pleasant for kids: chores, homework, being nice to their annoying siblings, and so forth. In these cases, parents resort to extrinsic motivation.

Extrinsic motivation is more complicated. It's what gets people to do things they don't find enjoyable. Extrinsic motivations lie on a continuum, with some being "better" and some being "worse" depending on how much they line up with the three basic psychological needs. Here are some examples of how people can be extrinsically motivated, from best to worst. Notice that the best ones still do a pretty good job of supporting people's autonomy, competence, and relatedness.

- You may do something because you believe it's important, even if you don't find it particularly enjoyable to do.
- You may do something because you believe it will help you achieve a different goal. For example, you might work out

3. Ryan and Deci, "Intrinsic and Extrinsic Motivation."

at the gym not because you love being sore and sweaty but because you want to be in shape.

- You may do something because you're pursuing a goal that's important to someone else—and you've convinced yourself that it's important for you too. For example, a middle school student pays careful attention to the latest trends because they want to fit in. Or perhaps a middle schooler who struggles in school is anxious to get good grades because their friends get good grades.
- You may not want to do this thing at all, but you'll be rewarded if you do it or punished if you don't. This is like when a seven-year-old might not be allowed screen time until they clean their room. Or perhaps you stay at a job that you hate, because it pays the bills.
- Last, there's *amotivation*, which means no motivation at all. In fact, the things that someone is doing to motivate you might have the opposite effect. For example, a bad experience with a math teacher could kill your desire to learn math.

People's motivation to work is usually mixed. This goes for both adults and children. The classic career advice is "Do what

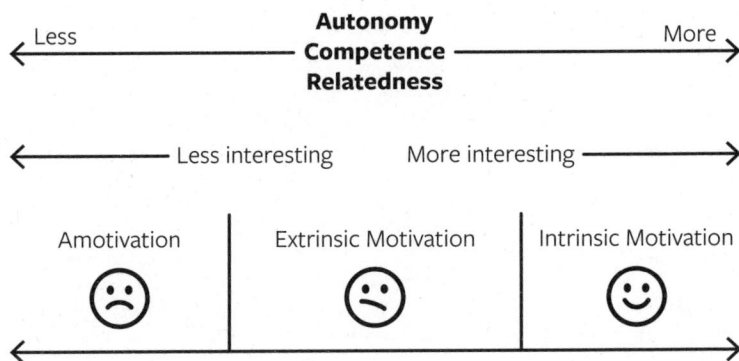

you love, and you'll never have to work a day in your life." But even when people have found their dream job, there are usually parts of it that are unpleasant. For example, I love my job teaching economics, but I don't love going to meetings and answering emails. When I look at why I do my job, I see many motivations.[4]

If we have a mix of motivations for tasks, we need a mix of strategies to make ourselves want to do them. Psychologist Lisa Damour argues that the tasks kids are asked to do are similar to food that they're given to eat. The kids might love the chicken nuggets and hate the vegetables. There's no shame in not liking the latter, but it's important that they eat both.[5]

Sometimes we expect kids to do drudgery that adults don't even like—namely, tidying up the house and cleaning up—and then wonder why they are unmotivated. You can't crowd out intrinsic motivation if there's none there to begin with. Of course, such drudgery still needs to be done. How can we help the kids get through that "plate of food"? We need to show discretion in how we use rewards and punishments.

What to Do

How do we do this as parents? We create an environment that supports our kids in the basic areas of autonomy, relatedness, and competence. A mini-economy can help with this.

4. As Richard Ryan, one of the founders of Self-Determination Theory, put it: "We almost always have multiple motivations for things that we do. Different levels of motivation coexist in almost every act. We have multiple motivations, but when some become dominant they can undermine the total quality of our overall actions." Scott Barry Kaufman, "Richard Ryan: Self-Determination Theory and Human Motivation," *The Psychology Podcast*, Sept 16, 2021, https://podcasts.apple.com/us/podcast/richard-ryan-self-determination-theory-human-motivation/id942777522?i=1000538281074.

5. Scott Barry Kaufman, "Helping Teens Thrive Emotionally and Socially w/ Lisa Damour," *The Psychology Podcast*, April 18, 2024, https://podcasts.apple.com/us/podcast/helping-teens-thrive-emotionally-and-socially-w-lisa/id942777522?i=1000652829428.

Let's start with *autonomy*. People do things autonomously when a task aligns with what they believe to be interesting and important. Remember how we talked about identifying our family values earlier? When we know what we value, we can use those values to set goals. According to psychologist Andy Yarborough, this value-based mentoring "is taking our children past obedience to understanding. Mentoring leads my children past the 'what' and into the 'why.'"[6] When kids understand the "why," they can grow in autonomy and therefore motivation.

A mini-economy is a great setting for autonomy support. Even if children don't want to do chores, it sets a "high floor" of motivation. Children may act like they have no inclination to do their work at all, but in fact they have some even if they don't know it. They chose their job in the first place, they understand why it's important, the rest of the family is working at the same time, they

THREE BASIC NEEDS

A simpler way to say "autonomy, competence, and related-ness" is "value, growth, and belonging." For me, the latter words are easier to remember and act on in real parenting situations. Ask yourself:

- Am I helping my children understand the **value** of the work or how it connects to values our family holds?
- Am I helping them keep a **growth** mindset—that is, understanding that their skills can improve with practice?
- Am I helping them feel that they **belong** and are connected to our family?

6. Yarborough, *Values-Based Parenting*, 23.

are exercising a special skill, they can take pride in their work, and through their income they can pursue other goals (by buying things). This doesn't describe a system of top-down control—it's a system in which children build autonomy by practicing making meaningful choices about money and work over time, guided by a values-driven mini-economy. They are growing.

Next, *relatedness*. In our family, we support this area with a Saturday morning meeting:

- We get to remind the kids about the value of their work.
- The kids get an opportunity to speak their minds.
- We set expectations.
- We can tell them how they can be successful.
- We review their savings goals and ask what they're interested in buying in the store.
- We remind them that the family relies on each of its members to make the house nice.

In other words, we support them in their basic psychological needs as those needs relate to chores. We avoid snuffing out whatever intrinsic motivation they may already have. We don't ask them to do pointless tasks, things that are purely drudgery (though some drudgery is OK), or things that isolate or shame them.

Try to create a family culture where kids understand and value the work that everyone does. Instill in them a growth mindset in which they can acquire and use skills. And let them know that the family relies on them and they rely on the family. This will give you a head start.

Finally, to support *competence*, don't forget to give the kids jobs that require skill. If they receive jobs that only require drudgery, all that's going on in their minds is drudgery. But if their jobs take creativity, then their minds will be on what they need to create.

For example, our eight-year-old Landscaper is constantly asking to use my power tools, like the edger, hedge trimmer, and reciprocating saw. It's a bit of a hassle for me, and frankly a bit dangerous for such a small child. I'd rather just do my job as Gardener and be done with it. Letting him use the tools requires that I give him safety training and then supervise him. It slows me down and makes me nervous that he'll get hurt. But what a great opportunity! He gains competence in several areas: using a new tool, learning safety guidelines, and knowing the kind of work that needs to be done to keep our yard nice. It also builds our relationship and his attachment to the work. He is the Landscaper, and Landscaper means competence.

That's why a mini-economy job should have a job title. It helps create an identity around the work a child does, and it signals that there is more to their labor than just "pick up your stuff." Before assigning kids jobs, think through what skills the kids might acquire over time that will help build competence and therefore attachment to the work. And then you can give them a raise!

"But hold on," you might be saying now, "what's this talk of giving them a raise? You haven't even proved that kids should be getting paid for their work at all!" I'm getting there. The point is that our motivations for doing chores are always mixed, but you can lay the foundation to support your kids' motivation to do them.

■ ■ ■ ■

Now we're ready to look at some findings about extrinsic motivation.

- Payment for a job can improve motivation. As Gagné and Deci put it, "Well-internalized extrinsic motivation appears to promote enhanced performance for aspects of people's work that are not interesting."[7]

7. Marylène Gagné and Edward L. Deci, "Self-Determination Theory and Work Motivation," *Journal of Organizational Behavior* 26, no. 4 (2005): 331–62.

- Money can be an effective incentive, but it sets a standard. If you pay the kids for chores, they're going to keep expecting to get paid. There's no going back. Don't assume that paying them for chores will "train them" to do them for free in the future.

- Payment is connected to feelings of competence. Payment for work supports motivation the most when it signals to the worker that they are competent.[8] That's why I recommend giving the kids a raise if they learn a new skill.

- Consistency is key.[9]

Many parents set up a two-tier work system in which kids *must* do some tasks for no money but *can* do extra jobs for money. I think this is a great method. This preserves the ethos of "you have to do this because you're part of the family." Paying them to do extra jobs—but not basic family work—teaches the connection between work and money, allows them to make their own choices, and keeps your house rules and expectations intact. Mini-economy jobs are good "extra work" on top of the basics like cleaning up after themselves or other family work that they must do.

If you refuse to pay your children for any work, you miss an opportunity to teach them about the connection of work to income. They don't get to practice connecting their work choices with their spending choices.

Again, a mini-economy is not a top-down system of rewards. It's an economy. Parents can set up a system in which kids are proud of their work and thoughtful about their financial choices.

---

8. Christopher P. Cerasoli, Jessica M. Nicklin, and Alexander S. Nassrelgrgawi, "Performance, Incentives, and Needs for Autonomy, Competence, and Relatedness: A Meta-Analysis," *Motivation and Emotion* 40 (2016): 781–813.

9. Melissa A. Lippold et al., "Day-to-Day Consistency in Positive Parent-Child Interactions and Youth Well-Being," *Journal of Child and Family Studies* 25 (2016): 3584–92; Michael Feehan et al., "Strict and Inconsistent Discipline in Childhood: Consequences for Adolescent Mental Health," *British Journal of Clinical Psychology* 30, no. 4 (1991): 325–31.

This system also fosters internal motivation and frees parents who feel stuck between the message that kids should be controlled with rewards and punishments and the reality that kids don't always want to do what they should and need some prodding.

Will the mini-economy wreck the kids' internal motivation? No. First, few motivations are purely intrinsic. For example, if you love owning a business, you likely enjoy not only the work but also seeing people buy and appreciate your product. If you love a particular sport, you probably enjoy winning more than losing. If you love volunteering, you still appreciate being noticed and thanked for your service. And it can all work backward too.

RULES OF THUMB FROM PSYCHOLOGICAL RESEARCH

1. First do no harm. Align tasks with values, and don't damage a child's sense of belonging or capacity to grow in competence.
2. Recognize and accept when a child doesn't like a task. Say "I know you don't like this," and work with them to find a values-aligned reason to do the work.
3. Listen and let them talk.
4. Having a good structure is valuable. It should provide predictable boundaries yet allow kids to make choices inside those boundaries.
5. Rewards can include a teaching function.
6. Rewards can be motivating if they're used properly in the spectrum of extrinsic motivation.
7. You can't damage intrinsic motivation if a kid has none to begin with. Sometimes people need to be given a reason to do something.

We may work a job for the money but still genuinely enjoy our time there. We may play a sport just to get in shape and also find ourselves loving the activity. We may do service work just for college applications but fall in love with the service and the cause in which we are engaged.

Second, giving rewards for work is something many parents are going to do no matter what. This book shows how to do it well—how to avoid the worst excesses of a token behavior management system while creating a home economy that preserves and builds internal motivation. There's a way to do this right.

Third, sometimes the children simply deserve to be paid. Some of the work that kids do around the house is actually valuable. The adults get paid for doing valuable work. Why shouldn't the kids get paid for their valuable work too? Fourth, extrinsic rewards don't have to inhibit internal motivation. They can replace lower forms of extrinsic motivation with higher, better forms.[10] And last, paying kids for chores teaches them about the connection between money and work.

So, should you pay the kids for doing chores? Here's the short answer: Pay them for some chores but not others. Some tasks should always be done as a minimum expectation, such as clearing their plate from the dinner table and putting it in the dishwasher and tidying up after themselves. But you should also give them the opportunity to do chores for money, whether it's mini-economy money or real money.

Now that we know what the research says about what, when, and how kids should learn about work and money, we'll continue looking at each part of a mini-economy: working, sharing, saving, spending, and making a business.

10. Ryan and Deci, "Intrinsic and Extrinsic Motivation."

—— THINK AND TEACH ——

Questions for Parents

1. What are some beliefs you have about money? Where did you get those beliefs?
2. If you had to change how you use money, do you feel like you could?
3. When you were growing up, how did your family talk about money?
4. What is something that's keeping you from talking about money with your kids?
5. If your kids were to do chores, what intrinsic motivations would they have? What extrinsic motivations?

Questions for Children

1. How do your parents pay for food at the grocery store?
2. Can we get everything we want at the grocery store? Why or why not?
3. What is a time that you've had to make yourself wait to get something you wanted?
4. If you wanted to buy something expensive, would you rather save more or work more?
5. What is some work that you enjoy?
6. Why might you get paid for some jobs but not others?

Lessons for Children

1. We can't have everything we want. But we can work to get the things that are most important to us.
2. Let's make a plan.
3. Choosing is refusing. When we choose one thing, we give up something else.
4. All our choices have costs and benefits (bad things and good things, risks and opportunities).
5. We can spend money on something small now or save for something big later.
6. We buy things with money, and we get money from working.
7. Our work helps others.
8. We work to make the things that we buy and trade with others.
9. Money makes trade easier.

PART 2

WHEN OUR FAMILY GETS MONEY

There is a lot of good advice out there on how to talk to your kids about money. The problem is, it is awkward to insert money talk into everyday life. Parents aren't always ready to do it, and kids need a more consistent structure for learning about money. Kids need a system in which they can practice using it consistently, both as consumers and producers. The next five chapters are about teaching kids how to get money (work) and "what our family does when we get money." Those are the magic words; they leverage the power of family identity to begin to instill principles of money management.

As we discussed in chapter 3, elementary-age children are ready to absorb money habits and values. (More technical money skills such as using compound interest are for the high school years.) Habits and values form the groundwork for budgeting later in life, but in a way, they are better than a budget because they determine whether a person will ever actually create and stick to a budget.

The classic budgeting plan for young kids is the Save-Spend-Share approach. I recommend this approach, but I've made one important change to it: I put sharing in first place rather than last. I will refer to the method as *Share*-Save-Spend from here on.

In the Share-Save-Spend method, children divide the new money they earn into three categories: one for sharing with or giving to others, one for saving for future spending, and one for spending immediately or before their next payday. Often, they have separate jars or some other container for each category—my kids made their own wallets out of paper.[1]

It's easy to see why so many personal finance advisers recommend Share-Save-Spend to teach kids about budgeting. We have been teaching our kids about sharing since they were old enough to say "mine!" And the spending part is easy enough to understand; it's what they really want to do. But we're trying to get our children to save money too. The Share-Save-Spend method helps us add that third category of saving and show our children they can actually plan what they will do with their money.

You can get them started by introducing the "Saving Plan" organizer chart you'll find in chapters 1 and 7. It helps children envision what they are saving for. You can also use it for family saving goals, which the kids save for with taxes and donations. In our family, when our kids earn their DayBucks, their first step is to give 10 percent to donations and 10 percent to taxes (or what we call "tithes and taxes"). I will discuss these in more detail in their respective chapters.

When you are done reading the next five chapters, you'll have new tools to round out your mini-economy. You'll also know more about what and how you will teach money skills as you go along. You'll invite your children to make meaningful choices about money over time. You'll "teach a kid to save." Let's get started.

1. For a great example of this in a children's storybook, see Tori Filas, *A Budget for Bingo*, illustrated by Ethan Roffler (Two Bunnies Press, 2024).

5

Working

The only thing harder than teaching kids about money is getting them to do chores.

Consider the following situation in my family. We didn't have a mini-economy going at the time; the kids were supposed to be following a simple "If you make a mess, you clean it up" rule. Easy, right? Here's what happened.

The kids had built a blanket fort in the little park across the street from our house. (Yes, it did make the park look like a campsite.) They had also set up a toy soldier battle in the living room. They were supposed to clean both of these up right after they were done playing. But the following problems intervened: They had soccer practice. Then they had homework. They also didn't want the fort and the battle to be taken down so soon, because they had "worked so hard to make them." (Come to think of it, they really know the kinds of arguments that will work on me.) Then they needed to bathe since they were dirty from soccer, so they could get to bed on time. Finally, they took down the blanket fort—in the dark—and threw all the blankets into our house's foyer. I complained that they had made a new mess, but they had already started their bedtime routine. The toy armies were still set in full battle array.

I did what many parents do in this situation: I mumbled to no one in particular that they should have cleaned everything up, tacitly admitted defeat, and put off the cleanup for later.

In "Chores," a chapter in *Fast-Forward Family*, Wendy Klein and Marjorie Harness Goodwin show how this experience is typical of middle-class parents who struggle mightily with getting their kids to do housework. Parents' attempts to get kids to do chores are frankly pathetic, as mine were in the story above. Parents plead, negotiate, threaten, nag, and finally just do the work themselves. They leave the situation feeling that their kids will grow up to have no work ethic.

But there is another dynamic at play. Klein and Goodwin also observed that "one of the biggest obstacles to getting children to help regularly with household tasks was lack of mutually agreed upon routines in everyday family life."[1] Parents often don't have a consistent vision or set of expectations for their children's housework. They prioritize other things above housework, particularly school and extracurricular activities. Kids are surprised when they are asked to do chores. The expectations simply aren't already in place. And then parents don't follow through. The result is that no one benefits. The kids don't do the work, and the parents feel bad for nagging.

As we learned from self-determination theory in the last chapter, people are motivated to do things both intrinsically and extrinsically. As Richard Ryan, one of the originators of the theory, put it: "We almost always have multiple motivations for things that we do. Different levels of motivation coexist in almost every act."[2] We are happier and more motivated when we have the internal drive to do tasks. But some tasks are just

1. Klein and Goodwin, "Chores," 118.
2. Kaufman, "Richard Ryan: Self-Determination Theory and Human Motivation."

no fun. Do *you*, dear parent, like to mow the lawn or scrub pots and pans? Chores are mostly this sort of drudgery. For unpleasant tasks, people often need some extrinsic motivation—rewards and punishments, carrots and sticks—as a boost to get the work done. The trick is to structure these incentives wisely so that they do not interfere with internal motivation and may even support it.

What to Do

To solve the housework problem, parents need to do three basic things—things a mini-economy system can help accomplish—that support the three essential ingredients for motivation discussed in the previous chapter: autonomy (or value-aligned-ness), competence, and relatedness. They are:

1. **Create a vision** and goals for why you're asking your kids to work. Get buy-in from the kids for that vision.
2. **Set expectations** for what work the kids should do.
3. **Insist on quality.**

Let's consider each of these in turn.

Create a Vision

This crucial first step of creating a vision and goals is what is often missing when parents try to get kids to do chores. When everyone in the family understands and even agrees upon the reason for chores, it supports all aspects of motivation. A shared vision makes the most of a child's desire for both independence and community, along with the desire to be good at something.[3]

3. Wendy S. Grolnick, Edward L. Deci, and Richard M. Ryan, "Internalization Within the Family: The Self-Determination Theory Perspective," *Parenting and Children's Internalization of Values: A Handbook of Contemporary Theory* 44 (1997): 135–61.

Why do you want your kids to work? If you need help answering that question, consider this list of possibilities:

- To learn responsibility.
- To contribute to the family.
- To get things done—I can't do all the work around here!
- To learn about why people work.
- To not grow up to be lazy.
- To appreciate work and the people who do it.
- To develop a good work ethic.
- I *don't* want them to do chores. I want them to play. Kids should play!

Or perhaps you want your kids to work because you feel frustrated. You see them sitting around doing nothing important while you are in the middle of a tough workday. So you suddenly tell them to get up and do a chore. Your requests are haphazard, not goal driven.

Let's find a better vision for chores.

If you haven't thought through what you actually want your kids' work to be for, then you might just be telling them to work because you're irritated. From your children's perspective, you don't seem to care whether they do chores—until you do. Then it's suddenly oh-so-important that they do work and do it now. This on-again, off-again approach simply doesn't function.

Instead, start with a vision for what work is for. Then build a system around that. The list below can help.

From my interactions with families, I've observed three main kinds of work that correspond to parents' vision for kids' work. The differences between them have to do with what the goal of the work is and whether kids are paid for it. If you teach them these categories, it will be easier for them to understand what the expectations for the work are. It's important to make these reasons clear and distinct, or kids will be confused about whether they should expect to be paid or not.

1. **Family work.** This is work kids are expected to do as part of the family, without pay. This includes cleaning up after themselves. As mini-economy parents George and Julie put it, "This is your responsibility. Part of living in a family, in a house . . . and being human."

2. **Service work.** This is work they do to help the community. It could be helping friends move, doing a youth group project, helping a neighbor, or participating in a school cleanup day. It's even better when it's consistently planned work or work done automatically. Planning service work for the family to do is a way to help build empathy, selflessness, and care for the community. Service work is also likely to come up at short notice, however. This means that it's sometimes difficult to set a consistent expectation for what the work will be. In our family, service work includes both neighborhood cleanup days and church service projects.

3. **Their job.** This is paid work. The money sends a message to the rest of the economy that the work is valuable and people are needed to do it. Paying kids to do chores teaches them about the value of work.

   Paid work can shift around more than family work does, but having consistent expectations children understand is key. It's best not to just announce out of the blue that you will or won't pay them for something. Make sure they know about their job ahead of time. Research shows us that once people are paid for work, they begin to expect it. If you want the kids to keep doing this particular work in the future, plan to keep paying them for it.

I mentioned earlier that mini-economy jobs should have titles. One reason is because it's the easiest way to tell them apart from family work; mini-economy jobs have job titles.

A mini-economy job is more than kids just cleaning up after themselves. These jobs make the house a better place to live in. Kids are more motivated to do their jobs and prouder about doing them if they know they're accomplishing something special that wouldn't be done without them.[4] Their work is making the family better off. This is part of the justification for paying them for their job: They're producing something new, and they deserve to share in the benefits it provides.

Set Expectations

As with so many other things in parenting, consistency is key for deciding chores for kids. A mini-economy isn't the only way to organize consistent expectations for work. But it is a way to make sure you *do* have consistent expectations.

Make sure you remain steady with any expectations for family work that kids already understand. Do not replace these with mini-economy jobs. For example, if kids have to tidy their rooms before they play after school, keep this rule in place. Mini-economy jobs are best for accomplishing new tasks. This is another help in maintaining the distinction between "family work" and "jobs."

When my wife, Sarah, and I first started doing a mini-economy with our kids, their jobs were optional. If they didn't want to do them, I said "No problem, but then I can't pay you." **I no longer suggest this.** They should do their jobs. This system thrives on buy-in from the family. The family does many kinds of interactions through the mini-economy that kids will miss out on if they aren't working and earning money. If you are building motivation using the techniques I discussed in the

4. Cerasoli, Nicklin, and Nassrelgrgawi, "Performance, Incentives, and Needs."

previous chapter, they will do their job (see "Insist on Quality" below for ideas on motivating recalcitrant workers). Maybe a mini-economy job could be something optional kids do for extra money, but in my experience that's a different thing. "Extra jobs" or "gigs" for pay are not a bad idea; they're just separate from a mini-economy.

Mini-economy jobs have a job title kids can understand. They can visualize the work. When my daughter Lucy was the Zookeeper, she knew she had to pick up stuffed animals (of which there were dozens) as well as fill the cat's food and water bowls. But since she understood that a Zookeeper takes care of animals in different ways, she also acquired a sense of responsibility for the cat. She would do little extra tasks, like letting him in and out and checking on his whereabouts.

Our mini-economy jobs list has also included drawings of the tasks that needed to be done. This was helpful when two of our four little workers were too young to read. It also made the list more cheerful and fun.

Whatever system you have for jobs, you can always leverage the power of belonging by having the whole family do their jobs at the same time. This makes the kids feel like they're part of something; it also makes it more obvious if somebody is slacking off. Plus, everyone can see the stark difference between before and after the work is done, which makes its value immediately obvious. Everyone works better when they feel like their effort makes a difference.

Parents are often anxious that their kids don't have a good work ethic. Don't despair. Setting up a system in which kids do housework isn't too hard. But as we have seen, parents often blunder around, unsure of what they want their kids to actually do. By thinking through the goals we have for our kids' work, setting expectations, and enforcing those expectations, work around the house doesn't need to be a negative experience for all involved. In fact, it can be fun and can help kids learn skills along the way.

Insist on Quality

It's also important to have consistent expectations of the quality of the work children do. This isn't just about having a nicer house. It's also about building skills, a sense of competence, and relatedness to the life of the family.[5] It will take longer to get the work done if you need to help kids get started with their jobs, show them how to do new things, model what a good job looks like, and make sure the work is done right, but it's worth it.[6]

When you first assign a job, you will need to work with the child to show them how to do it. This is important.

1) It demonstrates the level of quality you expect.
2) It teaches them a skill, which supports their feeling of competence.

You should set a time of day by which mini-economy jobs need to be finished. Insist that they finish their job and do it well. You shouldn't have to threaten not to pay them at all. Remind them why they are doing the work, starting with the reasons that best support internal motivation:

1) The family needs their help to keep the house nice.
2) They need the family in order to live in a nice house—the rest of the family is working too.

5. Christopher L. Loderup et al., "How Do Parents Teach Their Children About Work? A Qualitative Exploration of Household Chores, Employment, and Entrepreneurial Experiences," *Journal of Family and Economic Issues* 42 (2021): 73–89.
6. Ying-Chia Kao et al., "Preparation for Adulthood: Shifting Responsibility for Management of Daily Tasks from Parents to Their Children," *The American Journal of Occupational Therapy* 75, no. 2 (2021): 1–11.

3) They have the skill to do this job.

4) Doing a chore is nonnegotiable. If this particular job is not the right one for this particular child, you can renegotiate and retrain later. But not now.

And then, finally, end with these reasons:

1) They get paid. They have a saving goal to work toward.

2) The taxes they pay will contribute to the family treat.

Reinforcing the reasons that motivate them should get them working. You'll need to precheck their jobs before the deadline to let them know if their work isn't up to standard so that they'll have time to fix it. If they didn't actually do the job, don't pay them until they do!

If a child complains that they want a different job, tell them you can talk about that, but today they need to do the job as agreed. Talk with them later and discuss the alternatives. Most of the time, the child will have just been complaining and doesn't want to do any of the alternative jobs either! Getting them to agree on that particular job will help them feel responsible for it.

You don't need to keep up the same mini-economy system all the time. For several years, as I've mentioned, my family did ours only in the summer to help structure the time. During the school year, we do mini-economy less intensively and may even put it on pause. It is a tool, not a way of life. But you do need to maintain a consistent set of expectations for the work the kids do. Don't expect kids to do work for free that you've been paying them for. Mini-economy parents I've trained and spoken with report that the principles they've taught during their mini-economies stick, even when the system itself goes on pause. Children have learned skills they can keep using. They see the importance of the jobs they did and keep some ownership over them. They also learn the connection between work and the creation of value—that is, a nicer house. If you use a mini-economy not just to make them do work but to teach them about work, the lessons will stick.

What About Having a Job Checklist?

An alternative to a mini-economy job is an old classic: Pay kids for completing a checklist of regular tasks, such as making their bed, getting dressed, brushing their teeth, and getting ready for school on time. This is a good tactic if the kids have several regular tasks they (and you) need help organizing. The checklist is sort of like a to-do list. It makes things easier, as you don't have to actually give them mini-economy cash every time they do jobs. You can just keep a tally of their work and pay them on payday. But beware! Once you start paying the kids to do something, they'll expect payment to *ever* do it.

A jobs checklist is a time-honored way to organize kids' housework. But some experts, such as William Stixrud and Ned Johnson in *The Self-Driven Child*, say not to use one. Their logic is basically that any work on a jobs checklist is family work, and subjecting it to rewards and punishments can hurt children's motivation and autonomy. This makes some sense, and if anyone chooses to follow this advice, I would not blame them. But what if the kids' problem isn't so much motivation as simply remembering and keeping track of their daily tasks?

In this case I think a checklist can be a useful tool since it helps with structure and organization. A checklist is a good option when a child has a bundle of responsibilities that need to be done. The checklist replaces "reminding" kids—that is, nagging them to do work. In fact, if you find yourself nagging a lot, it might be because your child has too many tasks to do and needs to be nagged to do each one of them.

Instead, make a checklist of mini-jobs that need to be done. Pay the kids when they have done their entire list—not only part of it. For example,

- cleaning tasks (make bed, pick up toys)
- daily habits (reading, practicing musical instrument)
- being ready for school on time (backpack, lunch, water bottle, jacket, shoes on)

In the list above are nine mini-jobs. If you have two children and rely on personally reminding them to do each one, that's eighteen reminders per day, which is a lot of nagging. Replace reminding them with paying them, and your day will get mellower. Since the tasks are organized on the chart, you can wait until mini-economy payday to pay them.

They should get paid if they do their whole checklist well without being asked. But be careful: If you depend too much on paying them for regular behavior, you can run into problems when you end your mini-economy and they still expect payment. And checklist work doesn't bring the pride of workmanship that a job with a job title brings. The best mini-economy jobs are not for basic responsibilities but for some additional service that benefits everyone in the house and requires skill.

Because the goal here is as much about organization—both for the adults and the children—tell them that's what they're being paid for. Say: "Completing your chart keeps the house nice, and it also helps us all stay organized. That's why you're getting paid for this."

JOB CHECKLIST

Regular responsibilities are the first three tasks; extra jobs are the last two.

	Clean Room	Do Homework	Practice Piano	Extra Job 1	Extra Job 2
Stephen					
Peter					
Timmy					
Bubba					

Families often lack clear goals for kids' housework. Parents who set goals are more easily able to come up with expectations—but then these expectations need to be enforced. Household jobs are great for kids if you plan them well. They can do all the things on the "vision" list at the same time: build responsibility, learn to care about others and their surroundings, take the cleaning burden off Mom and Dad, accomplish things that might not get done without extra hands, and even develop family bonding and skill development. A mini-economy is a great way to start a work system if you don't have one already. And if you don't have one, now is the time to start.

■ ■ ■ ■

Are there other ways to have consistent work expectations if you're not doing a mini-economy? Yes. Lots. But each has benefits and drawbacks.

- **"Clean up your own mess."** This is one of the most familiar of all household systems. In fact, this is the system in our house right now since we've put the mini-economy on hold for the new school year. It has drawbacks. It requires parents to always be "on," keeping an eye on who is making which mess, and to ask the kids to clean up at arbitrary times rather than a set time. It causes arguments about who actually made the mess. The kids beg to leave their mess intact because they're "using it" (somehow they are always using it). Overall, I find the management of this system to be too difficult. But it's at least a system that makes intuitive sense.

  Note: Kids can have a mini-economy job and still have to clean up their own messes. In fact, I recommend this.

- **"You're doing this because you're part of the family."** This might be the most common philosophy I've encountered that's not based on allowance or rewards. But it always leaves me wondering what the details are of how children are motivated in this system. Are the kids rewarded somehow if they do their chores or punished if they don't? Is there a special family cleanup time? Does everyone jump into the same task or have their own individual jobs? Remember, the research shows that most middle-class families don't have a clear idea of the goal for chores or how to make children do their work. If you have a system for family housework, go with it. But make sure that "You're part of the family" isn't something you bark in frustration when all else has failed. That's not a system. That's an excuse.

- **Cleanup time.** There are certain times parents declare to be cleanup times. Our family sometimes uses this system. When we do, I declare a "Fifteen-minute clean." I tell the kids we all must work consistently and quickly for fifteen minutes. If we do that, the house will be clean and I won't bother them to do work for the rest of the day. This tactic has distinct advantages. Rather than enticing children with money, it leverages the family community as an incentive. It creates a kind of momentum and even camaraderie in the cleanup effort. It can sometimes even get everyone to work at a really fast pace, especially if it's even less than fifteen minutes. In fact, sometimes we do a five-minute clean. It's amazing how much better things can look in a short time. The disadvantages to this system are the randomness of the times that it's done and the inflexibility of the jobs. It's good for getting things picked up off the floor, for example, but not for more involved jobs that require skill, such as gardening (which was the mini-economy job done by our then-eight-year-old).
- **The internship.** This idea from parents George and Julie can be part of or separate from a mini-economy. Their

family shifted their mini-economy to the following work rhythm: During a certain time (a Saturday), Julie would work with one of her daughters on an "internship" in which she would teach her how to do a job that really took some skill. (Meanwhile, another daughter's job was to play with the baby.) The internship was an opportunity for individual attention—something often in short supply when a family has more than one child. It was a bonding experience. The child also got the pride of learning how to do something her siblings didn't know how to do while developing a useful skill. The internship also includes a time-delimited aspect that is similar to cleanup time in that everyone is doing housework together, which helps with motivation.

Eric and Theresa used an internship model to teach their eldest son to chop vegetables with "My big, scary knife, under supervision" (as Eric put it). And in our mini-economy, our two boys have learned particular gardening skills. Teaching children a special skill—especially one their siblings don't have—builds a sense of competence and can be a powerful motivator.

- **The procession.** For basic tidying, gather the whole family and lead them in a procession through the house, with everybody tidying and cleaning everything in sight as you go. You can choose a set amount of time to clean each location at which the procession arrives. This is a fun way to keep the whole family involved and moving while working.

- **Traditional housework.** We must not forget that families all over the world do not require a book on how to get their children to do housework since such work is simply part of the routine of daily life. The family goes about its business, and the kids are expected to jump in and do what the adults are doing. This is especially relevant in cultures where getting a college degree isn't seen as a fundamental and nonnegotiable part of growing up. Many readers of this book will have grown up in the traditional housework system, but in industrialized countries, this system is on the wane.

If you can create a family atmosphere where family members automatically do certain housework because it's just part of being in the family, well done. But many of us need help and clever ideas to set up a housework system. Just remember, if you're ever doing work around the house that takes some skill, invite your child to help.

Things to Add to Your Mini-Economy

- **Create a vision** and goals for chores.
- **Set expectations** for what work the kids should do.
  - Decide what family work, service work, and jobs kids should do.
  - Kids should only be paid for their jobs.
- **Insist on quality.**
- **A checklist can be helpful** if kids have many tasks to remember.
- **Make sure jobs require some skill.** Examples of skills kids can learn are fixing things, cooking, setting the table, arranging flowers, using garden tools, using appliances, decorating, changing filters, tuning up bikes, and pumping up balls. Think of things that might make you say "Just let me do it!" Then train the kids to do it!

—— THINK AND TEACH ——

Questions for Parents

1. Why do you want your children to have household jobs? What are some goals?
2. Should school be your child's job?
3. What chores did you have to do as a kid? What were your family's expectations when you were growing up?
4. What are your kids' chores? When are they supposed to do them? What happens if they don't do their chores?
5. What have you tried in the past that has worked? What hasn't worked?

Questions for Children

1. What jobs do you see grown-ups doing?
2. Connect job titles to the work people do. Ask the kids, "What does a _____ do?" You could ask them about the following jobs:
   - Teacher
   - Gas station worker
   - Doctor or nurse
   - Repair technician
   - Lawyer

- Economist
- Engineer
- Store clerk

3. Look at the job titles in chapter 1. Ask your children, "If we had a _____ worker in our house, what work would they do?"

4. Can you think of a time that you liked working on something?

5. If nobody in the world did any jobs, what would happen?

6. Which work makes us work the hardest? Family work, service work, or a job? Why?

7. What kind of work is most important? Family work, service work, or your job? Why?

8. If you could only play and never work, would you like that? What about if you only worked and never played?

Lessons for Children

1. People work to make things other people want.

2. In an economy, we trade the things we make for things other people make.

3. Money helps us trade the things we make.

4. There are two kinds of things we make with our work: goods and services. Goods are things we can touch. Services are when we help someone else. Does the work your mom and dad do provide a good or a service?

5. Some jobs are more interesting to do than others.

6. Work is sometimes enjoyable. We should look for jobs that we like to do.

7. We don't need to be paid to do things we like to do. We get paid for doing jobs that others won't do, can't do, or don't have time to do.

8. People need to learn how to do their jobs. School prepares us to do jobs. Some jobs take lots and lots of studying before people can do them.

9. People have different skills and interests that can make them better at different jobs.

6

Sharing

"Share!" is one of the first lessons we teach our kids, and it usually begins out of desperation. They're probably fighting over toys. In our better moments, we mentor them on the importance of being generous and thinking about others.

This is all fine until we bump up against a question about sharing that is tough to answer. For example, many busy intersections in our hometown of Richmond, Virginia, feature people with cardboard signs asking for handouts. The children are curious about this and ask why we don't give them money. Why don't we share?

"We do," I tell them. "Just not here and not in this way. Our homeless neighbors are made in God's image, just like us, and he loves them. But they usually have problems that need professional help. So we give to organizations that can help them better than we can."

Your answer might not be the same as mine, especially if you don't share my particular beliefs or you're not dealing with a question that's as visceral as the question of giving to homeless neighbors. But most parents consider sharing and generosity to be positive traits they want to teach their kids.

Here are some other ways you can explain giving in a more general way:

- "Neighbors look out for one another."
- "We have goals that are more important than just ourselves."
- "We want to help a cause we believe in."
- "We share because we want to help other people reach their goals too."

To teach kids about sharing, you will need to be able to explain *why* they should share and then teach them *how* to develop the habit of giving generously to causes they believe in. Giving is no different than any other area of responsible spending: If you don't make a plan to do it, it won't get done. It requires a plan that is based on your values. Let me propose two concepts that can guide you as you teach your kids money values:

Stewardship: the belief that resources should be used for responsible purposes.

Generosity: the willingness to give.

Stewardship

The study of modern economics is supposed to be value-neutral: You tell me your goal, whatever it is, and I'll tell you how to best get it. It wasn't always this way. The original Greek word *oikonomia* (economy) suggested the management of one's household resources *for the right reasons*. Resources were supposed to be used to help the community, to give generously, and to live wisely, not used for aimless luxury. *Oikonomia* was the management of resources for good.[1]

The Greeks also saw the world as a place of abundance, not scarcity. Nature gave food from the earth on which people could

1. Dotan Leshem, "Retrospectives: What Did the Ancient Greeks Mean by Oikonomia?," *Journal of Economic Perspectives* 30, no. 1 (2016): 225–38.

subsist. Sometimes it gave more than enough to live on. When it did, people were to practice *oikonomia* in planning how to use the surplus well.

Modern economic thought has several important advantages over that of the ancient Greeks. We now appreciate the importance of productivity: If we want abundance, it must come through human work and ingenuity. We also understand that no matter how wealthy we are, we still face scarcity in that we have tough choices to make. In fact, the more wealth we get, the tougher our choices become because we have better opportunities from which to choose. We face scarcity and abundance at the same time! To navigate this paradox, we return to the concept of stewardship, which calls us to make wise choices about our wealth.

The most common translation of *oikonomos* ("economist") in ancient Greek texts is *steward*. That means someone who wisely manages resources to good ends. This idea of stewardship grew over time in Greek culture. It eventually combined with Christian ideas of stewardship, which added the idea that everything belongs to God, and humans must look out for the things God has entrusted to them. Jesus taught that "You cannot serve God and money" (Matt. 6:24). In other words, we must use wealth as part of our service to God; we should not let concerns about money rule over us. The concept suggests that people should neither negligently waste money nor build their identity through piling it up or having a flashy lifestyle.

Money has a habit of taking wing if we don't plan how we will use it. We spend it on things that appear entirely necessary at the moment, but we still end up disappointed—and are left wondering where it all went. That's not using money well. Let's think about how to become good stewards.

Generosity

One way to steward our money well—to make sure it doesn't fly away—is to *plan for generosity*. Sometimes I look at my checking account and wonder where my money has gone. I'm not always happy with the result. But when I consider that I've donated money to causes I care about, I feel like I've accomplished something. I've made an investment in building or sustaining something that matters, been a part of creating a lasting legacy, and served my neighbors.

Donating money brings us many benefits:

- It prevents us from being miserable with money.
- It forces us to live within our means.
- It keeps us away from a mindset that always demands more.
- It shields us from life's uncertainties (because we're not living at the limit of our resources).
- It changes our hearts and molds us to care about the things we're giving to.
- It gives us a sense that we've accomplished something. We haven't frittered our money away.

But if we have no control over our money, we won't be able to give generously. So many of us don't have control over our money. Maybe we spend all of what we earn. We live right to the margin and don't have any money to give or to save. When life throws us a curveball, our finances are thrown out of whack, and that leaves us feeling more insecure than ever. It may seem strange to promise that giving money away can help with this, but it can. When we plan to give and do it consistently, it puts us in a more secure place. It takes the heart away from the constant dread of living on the edge and puts it in a place of generosity.

My friend Carl has been a financial planner for more than twenty years. The other day he told me, "I've been doing this a long time. Every single person or couple I've worked with who prioritizes *giving*, and lives on the rest, has believed it's worth it.

They may have other problems, but in the area of finances they have peace."

One thing is certain: We won't be able to share generously in a way that matters if we can't control our money. That's why it's important to build habits that help us control money, rather than have money control us.

◼ ◼ ◼

You can use your mini-economy to help your kids grow up to be generous adults. If you want them to practice generosity, I recommend making giving a must. But for it to be a "must," you need a "why." Why should the kids donate money? Be prepared to teach your kids why sharing is important. It will be rooted in what you believe is ultimately true, good, and valuable.

The value of *stewardship* leads to *sharing*. Sharing requires the value of *generosity*. And if one is to persist in generosity, generosity requires a *plan*. Therefore we teach our kids to budget their giving.

Our family helps the poor through giving to our church, which gives money to local charity partners and also provides us with opportunities to serve in purposeful ways. From time to time I take the kids on church service projects. They get to see that we put our work where our money goes. (This is an example of the service work discussed in chapter 5.) Since the kids know their work is valuable, they know that serving is valuable too. We might not be able to solve homelessness in Richmond, but we can show integrity by taking steps to care for our neighbors.[2]

If you seek to teach your kids to share, be ready to tell them why. Consider giving them opportunities to serve. Then help them build the habit of giving. They can practice this habit in the mini-economy.

---

2. I am aware of the many complications with charity work. This book doesn't get into the important questions about how to serve our neighbors well and without causing harm. For now, I'll just say that people should seek to learn as they plan to give. For a good resource from a Christian perspective, see Robbie Holt, Michael J. Rhodes, and Brian Fikkert, *Practicing the King's Economy: Honoring Jesus in How We Work, Earn, Spend, Save, and Give* (Baker Books, 2018).

What to Do

Donations

When you are preparing to do a mini-economy, before you have even started it, think about where your family should donate money. Perhaps you already have an organization to which you give. If you don't, you might have a cause your family cares about—find an organization that supports that cause and prepare to give to it. When you're introducing the mini-economy to the kids, tell them their work will help by sharing with the people who support that cause.

How does the kids' work actually support the cause? It doesn't provide any real new money to the parents to give, but cleaning the house is valuable work. The kids have helped with something parents would either have to do themselves or hire done. The parents are willing to pay a bit extra to have that work done by the kids. The kids' effort is ultimately the donation. Teach the kids that to donate means to share or give.

When mini-economy payday arrives, prepare to give first. (Remember, I'm assuming that both adults and kids have jobs and are getting paid.) Set an amount of money each family member must donate. I suggest 10 percent. As I mentioned earlier, during the summer our family members can earn up to 10 DayBucks a week (which makes the math easy), so we each donate 1 DayBuck per week.

This donation is the very first thing kids should do when they get paid. Set aside a location for the donated money to be stored (ours is a red box). When there is enough money saved up, parents will make a donation using the standard mini-economy exchange rate. For our family, since that's 1 US dollar for every 2 DayBucks, if we save up 50 DayBucks in our red box over the summer, we'll make an additional $25 donation.

As you prepare to do all this, ask yourself, *How do I decide what causes we'll give to?* This is where you refer back to your family values. What are some ways you and your family can be involved with helping those in need? When you connect real community service work to the money you give, it teaches a vivid lesson to a child, including "Not everything is about you." And you model it by showing that not everything is about *you*, the parent, either. Even as we all strive to earn, save, and spend money for the things we want in life, we must always look outside ourselves to something bigger.

This should be your first step once you've got your mini-economy up and running: Plan with the kids where their money will be donated. As your mini-economy matures, seek ways to get involved with the places to which you've donated. Many places need volunteers. This is a great way to get the kids more connected to the work to which they are donating.

We should teach kids that money gives us many opportunities to live well. They can learn that they do not need to fear the lack of money nor allow getting and keeping it to dominate their lives. They can be generous stewards.

Taxes

Taxes are one of the many options in the mini-economy for teaching lessons about life. How to include taxes: At the beginning of your mini-economy, when you ask your children which goals they'd like to save for, you can also tell them you must collect government taxes. In real life, the government uses taxes for things everyone in the community shares, such as roads, firefighters, and streetlights. You can add that these are things that would be difficult to provide by asking people to pay for them when they need them, as we do for items at the store. This is why the government provides these things using tax money. Citizens get a vote in how much they pay in taxes and how those taxes are spent. In the mini-economy, they will vote on a fun purchase the whole family will enjoy together. You can suggest you use your tax money to buy a treat the whole family can share (for example, doughnuts or a trip to an amusement park at the end of the summer). A lower weekly tax rate would cover the doughnuts (10 percent), or they could choose a higher rate to afford the amusement park (20 percent). Taxes can seem like quite a burden on kids' earning power on each payday, but paying them can lead to a fun family outing. And this exercise helps children see how many financial obligations grown-ups have in real life!

This last summer, our family had an ambitious goal for taxes: a big trampoline. The kids had been asking for one for a while. We decided as a family that we'd use our taxes to save up for one. This was a great use of the tax money. It was for the public good in that everyone got to use it. It was also expensive. In fact, the kids voted themselves a high tax rate: 2 DayBucks a week each! They were willing to burden themselves with higher taxes in order to get something we could all use that they really wanted. Sarah and I like having it because it's a great way to get the kids outside. "If you want to bounce on something, go bounce on the trampoline!" However, we did make a mistake with this: We allowed the kids to get the trampoline on credit because we wanted them to have it at the beginning of the summer (see chapter 10, "Mistakes," for more discussion).

■ ■ ■ ■

Start your teaching about money management with the lesson that we are stewards of the resources we have: We should use them wisely and be generous with them. Have the kids practice generosity by giving a portion of their income every week to sharing. They can also pay taxes. This isn't strictly necessary for the mini-economy, but we have found that it makes it more interesting and provides many opportunities for family discussion about money and how we use it.

Giving and taxes teach an additional important lesson about money management: In real life, we can't spend the full amount of our paychecks on simply buying stuff. We have responsibilities to the community. We need to plan for these responsibilities by setting money aside to make sure they get done. Sharing is a core responsibility and family value that should not wait until the rest of the money is spent.

Things to Add to Your Mini-Economy

- Talk about what sorts of community goals you want to help with or give to as a family.
  - If you already have some, talk about them.
  - If you don't have any, think about what you'd like to be involved with.
- Prepare to donate time as well as money.
- Remember that sharing is best done in the context of community.
- Use the "My Savings" chart to show progress toward saving for a donation.
- Set up a savings chart for the tax money that is building up to a family treat.
- When you've reached a sharing savings goal, make a real money donation! I suggest a conversion rate of 2 Bucks for 1 US dollar.

Saving Plan

Whose? _The   KIDS_

Draw your goal: ✏

Trampoline!

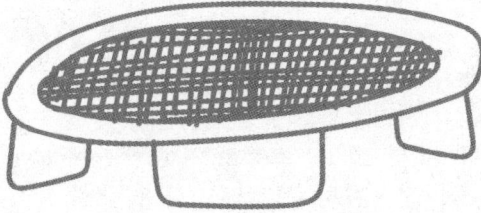

Today's Savings	Total Savings
6	24
6	18
6	12
6	6
6	0

Draw your 2nd choice
– what you give up ✏

(Store stuff)

Work to be done:

Our jobs + taxes

—— THINK AND TEACH ——

Questions for Parents

1. Are stewardship and generosity values you agree with? What is missing?
2. What good causes in your community would you like to support?
3. How is giving donations similar to investing? How is it different?
4. Is there a part of your budget you could adjust so you could donate more money?
5. Where do you donate your time?

Questions for Children

1. Why is sharing our money with others important?
2. Do we share all our money? Why or why not?
3. What would be a waste of money?

Lessons for Children

1. There are three things we do with money: sharing, saving, and spending.
2. Some things are more important than our own "right now" pleasure.

7

Saving

Saving summarizes all the principles of personal finance: Spend less than you earn, and the rest follows. Let's look at how it all works.

Think back to the beginning of the book, to the discussion of how we make choices. First, we look at our values. We decide what is important. This helps us know what to pursue and what to say no to. We seek to use money to support these values (stewardship).

Next, we use our values to set goals. Some goals are ultimate ("Love your neighbor"), some are big and important ("Give generously" and "Save for retirement"), and some are short-term and not very important but still kind of cool ("A USB-powered heated travel coffee mug? Buy with 1-Click!"). But they are all goals. Then we prioritize those goals by using our values as a reference. Sometimes we delay or even give up a goal in favor of a more important goal. For example, we can't save as much for retirement if we are clicking the Amazon button whenever we see something that promises to make our lives slightly more convenient. But we can't love our neighbors very well if we are always thinking about stacking up more money. Saving for retirement is a really important goal, but we might need to save less if we want to be generous (though we should probably be cutting spending, not saving). We organize our goals in order of importance.

We also don't reach our goals immediately. That takes time—and purposeful effort. Reaching our goals requires a plan. In personal finance, that plan is called a budget: giving, saving, and spending. Following our budget means we can't do whatever we want when we want to. We need to delay gratification. We need to discipline ourselves away from low-priority (but alluring) goals and toward high-priority but perhaps more distant goals. Planning means pursuing what we really want.

If we do all these things—find what matters, prioritize it, set goals, make a plan, and follow the plan—we'll get the things we believe truly matter. We won't fritter away our effort on lesser things.

Values → Goals (Prioritize) → Money Plan

Kids need to learn how to do these things too. Remember the central claim of *Teach a Kid to Save*: Kids need to practice making meaningful choices about money over time. This whole decision-making model is about helping kids extend their time horizons, delay gratification, and become wise choice-makers, even at a young age.

When I was sixteen, there was a day when a friend and I were sitting on our skateboards on a curb downtown. Suddenly my friend started. "Wait! I get paid tomorrow! I need to hurry up and buy something."

I looked at him curiously. "What does getting paid tomorrow have to do with buying something today?"

"I still have money," he explained, as if that answered the question. For me, it didn't, so I asked again.

He peered at me as if I was utterly ignorant of the principles of money. "I still have money left. I get more tomorrow. If I don't spend it all now, I'll still have money left over when I get my check."

The truth finally dawned on me. In his mind, all of one's money was to be spent before one got new money. The concept of saving was utterly foreign to him.

Saving isn't something that comes naturally to people, especially to kids. They have to learn about it and develop habits for doing it.

Saving is really just spending we put off until later. Whatever we buy later as a result of saving is usually better than something we would have bought without saving. Why? Because saving allows us to get things that are more valuable. It shows what delayed gratification is all about: achieving more important goals by giving up smaller, less important goals (such as momentary comfort).

Another important benefit we get through saving and delayed gratification is increased financial stability, peace, and freedom. Being under financial stress—not being able to make payments, such as in a financial emergency, or not being able to afford things that are genuinely special to us—is one of the worst feelings. It is even bad for our health. Having money saved allows us to move through life with a lighter load. One of the reasons for this financial freedom is that if we save, we have also trained ourselves not to need so many material comforts. It's a double bonus. Financial freedom is a great feeling.

Paradoxically, those who save also get to spend more in the long run (especially when saving brings compounding interest and market returns, which we won't get into here). So disciplining consumption isn't actually about having smaller desires. It's about having *better* desires. It's about giving up not-so-important things in exchange for more important things. It's about organizing our priorities.

What to Do

Remember how at the start of the mini-economy I encouraged you to sit down with your children and ask them what sorts of goals they'd like to save up for? When they save, remind them that they're getting the money for the thing they really want. This helps you not seem like you're just harping on them to give things up. Having lots of money, after all, is not the goal of saving. The goal is to spend our money on something important or to be financially free—that is, to have money to spend when we need it.

Some kids will be good savers, and others not so much. If you are concerned that your children won't understand or value saving, it's OK to set a mandatory weekly saving rate. You could set this amount low (20 percent of their earnings) or high (50 percent or even higher). Setting money aside for something right when they earn it communicates the value of saving similarly to how we earmark money for sharing. Mandatory saving teaches the lesson that it is a normal, important part of everyday work and earning.

My children all took different approaches to saving when we began. Daisy had been learning about patterns in school, so she wanted her saving and spending to form a pattern. I don't remember exactly what the amounts were, but it was something like "Save 5 DayBucks one week and spend 3; save 3 DayBucks the next week and spend 5." I'm not sure how rational this was from a budgeting perspective, but it allowed her to apply a lesson from school on quantitative reasoning (patterns) to the mini-economy, so we went with it. Calvin had a more conventional approach: He noted something he wanted to buy—he went straight for a toy—and diligently saved almost all his money for it. He gave up a lot of small, short-term things for the sake of that toy, including the clip art printouts he had been constantly badgering Sarah for. (This was a win-win for all of us. By sacrificing printouts for the toy, he got a truer understanding of the value of both. Showing the value of trade-offs is something a market economy does very well. And it kept his mom from having to make a million copies.)

Robbie, who was four at the time, was more interested in buying candy and lemonade, at least at first. But as weeks passed and he saw how his older siblings were saving, he wanted to imitate them.

So he, too, was able to save and eventually had enough to get a toy at the end of the summer. Both boys ended up spending their savings on mutant animal warrior toys, and there was much rejoicing.

Ways to Save

Where does this "saved money" actually get saved? Here are a few options:

- **Use the "My Savings" template** in this book. The kids draw their savings goal on it and then fill in how much they've saved toward it. They can make new charts for each new thing they're saving toward. And better yet, they can also use charts to visualize their tax money and donation money being saved. This gets them in the habit of seeing all money as needing to be saved toward a particular goal, which in turn helps with budgeting. They're learning so many things at once!

COLLEGE SAVING

You can add a lesson about the real world by giving kids the option to save for college. If they learn a new skill and save up a certain amount of money, you can give them a raise. College saving can be another thing they have to save for each week. (Yes, they will notice how many things there are to save for!) Use this idea to discuss education with them. Research shows that kids with any amount of money saved for college are more likely to go to college. This gets them thinking about it early. See chapter 12, "What Comes Next," for further discussion.

Saving Plan

__Riley's goal_____

Draw your goal: ✏️

SK8!

Today's Savings	Total Savings
8 extra job	38
4	30
4	26
10! Birthday	22
4	12
4	8
4	4
	0

Draw your 2nd choice
– what you give up ✏️

Work to be done:

Gardener

- **Piggy bank.** This is the classic option. It doesn't even need to be a pig! In fact, decorating a "money box" can be a fun activity to kick off a mini-economy, especially for small children. And making their own money box can motivate them to save.
- **Digital banking simulation.** There are several good ones online. Once you really get going with digital banking, it's one of the easiest options since you can have the bank automatically pay the kids each week. Of course, this means the kids might not get to see or handle their money, which can make the experience less vivid. A good option is to begin with cash only and then transition to an online option if you want to.
- **Money book.** That is, a ledger. Our children have made little folders out of paper that have pockets to store money and sheets of gridded paper to keep track of their funds. When we pay them, they keep track of their sharing, spending, and saving in their money books. We call this "accounting." You can use the accounting sheet included here. Some benefits of this approach:
  - Keeping track of money with accounting has several benefits. Accounting teaches real-world math skills.
  - The kids *will* lose their money. Sometimes seconds after they get it. Accounting can be a lifesaver when you need to find out how much they should actually have.
  - Accounting teaches kids the importance of recordkeeping.
  - Accounting helps you eventually teach about more complicated aspects of money such as online banking, credit cards vs. debit cards, and even cryptocurrency. This is because so much of the financial world simply involves different ways to keep records of money. Personally, I

didn't set out to teach my kids these things, but sometimes they ask! For example, my kids wondered why I swipe a card or tap my phone at the grocery store instead of paying money. I told them, "When I tap my phone, the bank erases money from my accounting sheet and puts it in their accounting sheet."

Let's consider an example in which Julia earns 10 Bucks each week. (You can find a full-page money book template at the end of this chapter.)

JULIA'S MONEY BOOK (B = BUCKS)

Date	A: Beginning Money (last week's money saved)	B: Money Earned	C: Money Shared	D: Money Spent	E: Money Saved (A + B – C – D = E)
July 10	0 B	10 B	1 B	4 B	0 + 10 – 1 – 4 = 5 B
July 17	5 B	10 B	1 B	0 B	5 + 10 – 1 – 0 = 14 B

We had our kids keep money books for our first few summers doing mini-economy, but after a while it started to feel cumbersome. The kids didn't want to do the math, and neither did we. So we just counted on them keeping track of their money and let that be sufficient.

It wasn't. They lost their money and routinely forgot how much they had (we weren't keeping a savings chart either). The mini-economy still worked fine, but we had to navigate several crises when kids lost, switched, or dubiously claimed money. And they missed the opportunity to visualize how much they had saved. Accounting for money is an important learning opportunity. I recommend a money book or savings chart.

When we started our mini-economy for the first time, I taught the kids about reaching their goals before I taught anything else. But I taught it in two ways:

- To get the things we want, we need to give up other things we don't want as much.
- To get the things we want, we need to save.

Of course, these are both just aspects of saving: There are trade-offs. The thing is, my two eldest children—then six and eight years old—each took a different lesson to heart. When we revealed our household store, I asked each kid what they wanted to save for. Here's how it went.

"So, Calvin, you could spend your money on screen time, fire, printouts—*Robbie!* Do not *eat scissors*, child! Give me those—treats, or a toy. Which would you like?"

[Calvin points at the toy.]

"The toy? That's the most expensive thing, so will you be able to get these other things if you're saving for the toy?"

[Calvin shakes his head no.]

"Good," I said. "Now, Daisy, what would you like to spend your money on?"

"I think all of them," replied my then-eight-year-old.

"So, what will you have to do if you want all of them?" I asked.

"Save save save save save save!" she exclaimed with a wag of her finger with each "save."

Notice my mistake. I had told Calvin that he had to give everything else up, but I told Daisy she could get everything if she saved. Calvin desired justice.

"Does Daisy get the most expensive one?" he piped in his tiny voice.

"Yes, but she'll have to save the most too," I replied.

This was all on video, and I noticed later what had happened. I had stressed trade-offs for Calvin but saving for Daisy. I don't think the outcome was bad. They both quickly noticed that saving for the expensive toy required giving up the smaller things in the store. But even at age six, Calvin was alert to the mechanics of planning and saving. Though I'd made a mistake explaining it, the mini-economy system fixed things, since once we actually got started the kids had a way to easily apply the lessons I was trying to teach and could see that saving and delayed gratification were part of the same thing.

As I have said, saving is just a plan for spending later. The money still eventually gets spent. The wonderful part of having a plan for your money (budget) is that once you've paid your fixed costs (giving, taxes, and saving) you are free to burn through that spending money with no guilt.

But most importantly for your kids, saving forms a habit. It teaches them that they need a plan for their paychecks and they need to delay gratification. It also teaches that they really don't have as much money as they think they do, once they factor in sharing, saving for emergencies, and saving for big ticket items. These are the money values and habits they will carry with them into adulthood.

Things to Add to Your Mini-Economy

- Ask the kids what they'd like to save for. Is it something in the store? Or something else they've discussed with parents?
- Set up a savings chart for each kid's saving goal.
- Don't forget to make your own savings chart, parents! The more you participate in the mini-economy, the better the family conversations will be.
- Adults should save their money for things kids make in their mini-economy businesses (see chapter 9).

—— THINK AND TEACH ——

Questions for Parents

1. Do all the adults in the family share a vision for saving and spending? If not, where can you find common ground? (*Note: I bring this up with some hesitation, but this is important. Money values are one of the main things that cause friction in a marriage. The good news is that coming to an understanding about family finances can reduce that friction. If you don't have a common vision, then you have identified something to work on as a couple.*)
2. What makes it difficult for you to teach your kids about saving?
3. If you could cut some spending, what would you save for?
4. If you could spend some of the money you've saved, what would you spend it on?
5. Which of your kids is a saver? Which is a spender? What money habits do you see beginning to form in your kids?

Questions for Children

1. Why do we save money and not just spend it all right away?
2. Do you like saving money? Or would you rather just spend it right away?
3. Is saving hard for you to do?
4. What things do you think grown-ups save for?

Lessons for Children

1. Saving is just a plan to spend later.
2. We save for emergencies and to get big things later.
3. If we keep track of our money in a money book, then we know how much money we are supposed to have in our piggy banks.

_____'S MONEY BOOK

Date	A: Beginning Money (last week's money saved)	B: Money Earned	C: Money Shared	D: Money Spent	E: Money Saved (A + B − C − D = E)

8

Spending

Now is the fun part! The kids get to spend their hard-earned mini-economy money at the household store. My family sets up our store on the kitchen table and populates it with goods (e.g., candy and toys), as well as homemade coupons for other goods and services (e.g., go to a Richmond Kickers soccer game with Dad). Our family has Store Day every Saturday, directly after the kids do their jobs, get paid, and manage their money. (Because of course they must share and save before they spend.)

I'm writing an awful lot about planning in this book, and that's intentional. For adults, a budget is a spending plan. It's how we manage our money. It helps us fulfill all our responsibilities. In parenting, a spending plan has an extra benefit: If the kids know that spending must be planned for, they learn not to expect impulse buys. Developing a habit of only spending money that you've planned to spend makes your parenting life easier. When I was a kid, I never, *ever* expected my parents to buy things on impulse. They had trained me too well. (Of course, I was their first child and they just didn't have much money. I believe my little brothers were spoiled by heaps of random luxuries!)

131

What about spontaneity? Are we taking the spice out of life by removing spontaneity from our spending decisions? If being spontaneous is one of your goals, you'll need to plan for that too. A person who wants to be spontaneous should save more money, not less, so that when interesting opportunities pop up, they have the money to take advantage of them.

From a parent's perspective, the best part of kids' spending in the family store is that it can keep them from begging you for things. What they buy is their choice. They did the hard work to earn the mini-economy money, so they deserve to buy something. Furthermore, you've guided them to a responsible plan for their money. Just as saving gives financial freedom because you have enough to spend when you need to, budgeting allows you freedom in spending because you know that you've already met your obligations.

A mini-economy should give children the opportunity to buy things that they would not usually get (or at least not as many as they would like). For example, I am happy to take my kids to watch local pro sports, but it can get expensive and it keeps them up late. Letting them buy a coupon to go to a game keeps it in the "treat" category.

It's fun to see the different approaches children take to spending. You'll probably learn something new about your kids as well. As I mentioned, during our first mini-economy summer, our oldest child arranged her spending habits in a pattern as a goal in itself, our next child hoarded all his money so he could personally clean out the store at the end of the summer, and our third child saw the store as a way to ensure a steady supply of chewing gum. When our youngest child (age four at the time) joined the mini-economy, she agonized over every saving and spending choice each week.[1] However your children choose to spend, you can bet it will give

1. Lucy has since overcome this ambivalence. She now spends enthusiastically whenever she has the money. "Daddy, I'm fine with this life," she explains. She is *six*.

you some insight into their personalities. And it gives you a great place to start conversations like the ones suggested at the end of each chapter.

Letting kids buy things they don't always get sends the message that the work they do is *productive*—it creates new value. This separates a mini-economy from a mere behavior management system. A mini-economy allows them to enjoy the fruit of their labor, not simply get rewarded for obeying rules (though they should still obey the rules).

What to Do

Over time, I've learned that coupons for privileges are the best thing to sell in the household store, rather than goods from the (real) store. This is for several reasons:

- I don't want my house cluttered with more plastic junk.
- Privilege coupons provide a way to manage all the requests the kids bug you with. Whether you say yes to this or that doesn't need to just be a function of your mood.
- Coupons don't get old and boring. Kids always want an "Ice Cream Trip with Mom" coupon. But if they don't buy the book or card game you put in the store, it stays there forever.

I have also found that the best goods to allow them to buy are those things you usually say no to because they are expensive, inconvenient, or contain too much sugar. The kids have to buy them with their own mini-economy money, which is limited, so you won't be overwhelmed by the expense or inconvenience—and they won't be overwhelmed by the sugar.

For example, as I mentioned earlier, when our son Calvin was six, he loved to color clip art images that my wife printed from the internet. But it quickly became apparent that these printouts were bringing us a large expense and hassle. They cost ink, paper, and, most importantly, time, since Sarah had to click through dozens of images to satisfy his demand for different pictures. When we started our mini-economy, we allowed him to buy clip art printouts. Faced with this cost, he scaled back on the number of printouts he needed and started drawing his own pictures from scratch instead. Before we did this, Sarah had borne all the cost of the printouts; now Calvin had to share it too.

At your store, allow the children to gobble the candy they bought right then and there, if they so choose. Go on the special outing at the first opportunity when they ask for it—don't make excuses about how "Mom and Dad are tired from work." That is probably true, of course, but the kids earned that outing fair and square, and it's time to reward them.[2] And if they've saved up enough to buy a toy but bedtime is getting close, maybe let them stay up a bit later so they can play with it. Store Day is like harvest season, a time for celebration!

The thing you do *not* want to do is to make the children pay for things you usually give them for free. That would make the mini-economy a net negative in their lives—a punishment. For example, I usually take the kids on an "adventure" on Saturday mornings while Sarah rests. Since these adventures are routine, making the kids pay for them would seem like a punishment. Furthermore, they wouldn't all choose to pay for them, which would compromise Sarah's rest time.

"Adventure with Parent" coupons can be tricky. The rule of thumb is that you should only sell coupons for things that are truly extra—things that kids either wouldn't usually get or would get only in limited quantities.

2. Calvin wanted our adventure to be "playing war" at the Petersburg National Battlefield. Thus I found myself pointing a stick at him and shouting "Bang!" at a reconstructed Civil War fort near the site of the Battle of the Crater, to the concern of onlooking tourists and the displeasure of the park rangers. It was embarrassing, but I had to respect the Adventure Coupon.

Don't underestimate the power of coupons for privileges. I experienced this personally as a child. When my mom and dad set up our household mini-economy, some of the first items I bought were coupons to "Go on a run with Dad" and "Go on a bike ride with Dad." Dad was happy to go running with me. But then my brothers also wanted to go, so they demanded our mother make more coupons for the store. She was happy to oblige; it got the whole family out of the house and gave everyone (else) exercise. After a few days of this, however, my dad complained that he was being run ragged, and my mother duly increased the price of the coupons and limited the amount offered for sale. But I think my parents counted the whole idea as a success.

Sarah and I started our mini-economy using similar coupons. The kids liked buying them because they could dictate how the one-on-one "adventure" went and didn't have to negotiate with siblings and parents about what activities to do. But after a while it felt like we were making them pay for quality time, and I made two changes. First, I make sure to schedule one-on-one time with each child. That's not part of the mini-economy; it's just something I owe them as a parent. We have four children, so this takes some planning. However, they value it so much. They love time with their siblings, but they feel really special to get focused one-on-one time.

Next, I still sell one-on-one adventure coupons that come with a treat. For example, when Robbie was eight, he started asking to go to US Best Wings, a grungy takeout restaurant that had recently opened in our neighborhood. He thought the large pictures of food they had in their windows looked good, and he'd caught me with a US Best Wings bag in the car. None of the other kids wanted that—they'd stick to hot dogs and chicken nuggets if they could, while Robbie had more cosmopolitan tastes. So I sold him a coupon to get the restaurant food he wanted and an adventure of his choice.

Be careful in deciding what coupons to make. When in doubt, talk about it ahead of time with your spouse and even with the kids. We will continue selling Adventure with Parent coupons on Store Day, but I make sure to give plenty of adventures for free. If they buy a coupon, it's basically to overcome a "not now" from me.

Troubleshooting Your Store

It's best to sell all goods and services at the store and not to make up prices for things as you go through the week. For example, if a child is demanding something, don't just say "Well, you can have it for 5 Bucks." Rather, say "We can make a coupon for that so you can buy it in the store. But we're not going to do that right now."

Think twice before selling privileges that may inconvenience the other children rather than the parents, such as a coupon that allows a child to choose what show to watch. In this case, the other children bear the cost of their sibling's purchase. This also runs the risk of upending whatever rules you had in place for who gets to choose the show, which can seem like an injustice to the other siblings. Remember, mini-economy purchases are supposed to bring new items and privileges to the kids, not redistribute items and privileges among the kids.

On the other hand, you can't entirely avoid provoking some envy. Sometimes a child will consume candy that they bought quickly but then have to watch while a more patient brother or sister consumes their candy a few days later. Sometimes they get buyer's remorse. Or they may feel bad that they don't get a sleepover while their sibling does.

That's OK. An important part of mini-economy is teaching your children the power of their choices over time. When they feel the "pinch" of their buying decisions, they learn to make a tight connection between working, saving, buying, and consuming. They learn that their choices matter. And they learn when to wait and when to act on buying and consuming the things they want.

Sometimes parents will notice that items in the store have been mispriced. For example, we had coupons for lemonade in our store, and when those proved popular, I became worried about the children's sugar intake. If something like this happens, wait until the following week to raise prices; don't raise the price then and there while the kids are still shopping. It is probably generous in this event to also lower the price on something else so the kids don't feel that, like Lucy and Charlie Brown, you're "yanking the football away."

EXPANDING YOUR MINI-ECONOMY

OK, you have an idea of how to get started with your mini-economy. But now it's time to go deeper. A mini-economy gives you all sorts of possibilities for teaching your kids about the world they live in. If you are getting more comfortable with your mini-economy and want to do more, what features can you add? Here are a couple ideas:

Scholarships. Award the children scholarships in which they get mini-economy money for reading books, doing art projects, or some other academic activity. You can review their scholarship at the end of a month to see if it will get renewed.

Selling insurance. Selling insurance in your store is a way to teach kids about risk. Include low price insurance coupons for sale. Tell them that sometimes we break our things. They can choose to try hard not to lose things, but they can also buy insurance. If their toy gets broken, they get a partial refund if they have insurance! For more fun ideas about teaching kids about insurance, look up my post on *Paper Robots* titled "Why Are Insurance Ads So Weird?"[1]

1. Stephen Day, "Why Are Insurance Ads So Weird?," *Paper Robots*, October 22, 2024, www.drstephenday.com/p/why-are-insurance -ads-so-weird.

Some big-ticket items may require kids to save up. This might be an expensive toy but could also be a coupon for a trip to the trampoline park or laser tag facility. You should talk these over with your kids ahead of time to help them set their goals. In some cases, the high-price experiences will be worthwhile things you want the kids to have, like an annual pass to the zoo, children's museum, or botanical garden. I have personally found that the kids will be happy to have *you*, the parent, buy these expensive passes but will value them only so much. As their parent, you probably have a good guess how much. One option in this case is to have the kids pay a certain amount toward the cost of these in mini-economy money. (If the kids are older, perhaps middle school age, they can pay in real money.) The nice thing is that you can consult with them about setting a fair amount for them to pitch in. This helps them build their sense of autonomy, think about how much they value the experience, and decide whether they want to help pay for it. People make better choices when they can feel the effect of those choices.

Store Day is a day to celebrate. The kids have earned what they buy. They've been responsible in putting their money where it ought to go. The money they have left is money they can spend. And spend they should. Let them know that they can freely spend the amount they've planned. You've taught them they can feel good about how they use their income when they plan to use it well.

One last tip: We've had a problem with the kids getting bored of the store. It just had the same stuff in it week after week. The kids still wanted the coupons for privileges—those never got old. But the games, books, stuffed animals, and the like that didn't sell early tended to sit around. Maybe this wasn't so bad. After all, we didn't really want the kids to get more hunks of plastic to sit around the house, ignored, while the kids say "I'm bored! There's nothing to do!" But it does seem important for there to be a bit of excitement come Store Day.

As we go forward, I plan to keep the store fresher. I will put out fewer things to begin with and have some in reserve. That should help keep their interest. I am also reminded to lean in to the lessons in the previous chapters on sharing and saving: to emphasize to the kids that we're giving to causes we care about (and volunteering for them) and saving for bigger goals. The things in the store are sometimes just a distraction from those other goals.

I hope that as your kids grow through your mini-economy, they'll start to view consumption in this way. "When our family gets money," they will know there is a lot to do with it. They must plan to share some, pay some in taxes, save some for their goals, and spend some on weekly priorities—and then they can spend some on something fun in the store. Most of the money they get can't be spent willy-nilly, which is just like real life. They will develop good money habits as participants in an economy in which they are stewards of resources that are meant to be used wisely.

Things to Add to Your Mini-Economy

- Make sure your store is well-stocked with fun items and coupons for privileges. Plan to add things to the store periodically.
- Put lower prices on things you want the kids to have (books) and higher prices on things you don't want them to have (plastic toys).
- As the mini-economy continues, plan to put things on sale, expand the store, and ask kids what else should be in it. The store needs to be fresh if the kids are to remain interested.
- Remind kids that saving is just spending later for something better.
- Try not to randomly charge kids for things. Plan ahead. Make coupons.

—— THINK AND TEACH ——

Questions for Parents

1. Do you have a plan for saving and spending your money? What makes it hard to plan?
2. What money habits did you grow up with?
3. What spending habits do you want your kids to have?

Questions for Children

1. If you had your own money, what would you want to spend it on?
2. Is there anything in the family store that you really want? Anything that you don't care about?
3. What are some goods you want to buy? Services?
4. Why is it important to have a plan for spending money?
5. How did you think of your spending plan?

Lessons for Children

1. If we spend all our money, we can buy little things.
2. If we save money for later, we can buy bigger things.
3. We can mix saving and spending.
4. It's good to have a plan for what we want to spend money on.
5. If we don't have a plan for our money, we may get upset later when we can't get what we want.

9

Making a Business

The TV show *Bluey* has an episode titled "Markets."[1] In it, the main character, Bluey, is sad that she has spent all her money from the Tooth Fairy on something she didn't end up liking very much (a toffee apple).

"Dad, I'm not sure I made the right choice," she tells her father. "Can I get my five bucks back? I think I want to put it in that [guitar] case and buy a song."

"That's not really how it works, kiddo," he replies. "Once you spend money it's, well, gone."

"Don't worry, Bluey," her friend Indy tells her. "As my mama always says to me, what goes around comes around."

"What does that mean?" Bluey asks.

"I dunno." Indy shrugged.

The next scene demonstrates what it means when money "goes around" and "comes around" as it follows the progress of the five dollars as it makes its way through the market. The money gets

1. *Bluey* is a cartoon show for kids about a family of anthropomorphic dogs. See *Bluey*, episode 49, season 2, "Markets," 4:40, directed by Richard Jeffery and written by Joe Brumm (Australian Broadcasting Corporation, October 25, 2020).

passed from stall to stall as each vendor gets the money when they sell something and then uses it to buy something else in turn. Eventually, the money is spent at Indy's mom's booth where she sells gluten-free cake. Indy's mom gives the money to her daughter, so she can spend it on exactly what the girls wanted—a song request. The money the girls had spent flowed through the market until it came back to them.

This scene perfectly shows how an economy flows. On one hand, once you spend money, it's gone, just like Bluey's dad said. On the other hand, we are all interconnected. Everyone is both a buyer and a seller, a consumer and a producer. What we put into the economy, we get back out of it. A market economy is a network of people making trades with one another. In each trade, both sides expect to benefit.[2]

Your kids can experience a market economy in a small but meaningful way if they start businesses in your mini-economy. Sure, you can start a mini-economy without the kids making businesses. But I highly recommend they do eventually make businesses and sell what they produce on Store Day. Selling to their family takes their learning about money to another level, for reasons I'll explain in this chapter. And besides, it's more fun.

Why Are Markets Important for Teaching Kids About Money?

A market is a place (or situation) in which people buy and sell goods and services. A market solves a puzzle that all economies must solve: What do we produce, and how much, and for whom? More importantly, how do we *know* that we're making the right choices for these things? A market does this by taking the combined knowledge of everyone in the marketplace and communicating it to everyone else through special information called *prices*. Prices

2. Alexa M. Quinn, Stephen Day, and Lauren Shifflett, "*Bluey*-conomics: It's Not All About the Money," *Social Studies and the Young Learner* 37, no. 4 (March/April 2025): 26–32.

tell both consumers and producers when something is scarce or when it is plentiful. When something in the world changes, prices change with it.

Coordinating the economic actions of billions of people is a more difficult puzzle than we can imagine. We take the puzzle-solving power of prices for granted. It seems logical for us that grocery shelves should be stocked with the food we like, the stores should have the clothes we want, and quality services should be available when we want them done. But in fact it's a societal miracle.

When kids get experience running a business, even a play one, they begin to understand what a herculean task it is for businesses to provide goods and services to consumers. Resources aren't freely available—they are scarce. And the money they get for selling something isn't pure profit—there are costs to cover. They can't just amuse themselves—they have to cater to the desires of others. And, perhaps most astonishingly, their choices matter. This isn't a top-down system in which adults tell them what to do. The kids get to be the deciders. Their choices are powerful.

When my little brother Peter was six years old or so, he started a business. But it was a scam. He made a grocery store using items from our fridge. He simply pulled things out of the fridge, put them on the kitchen table, and made cute little labels with prices. Five cents for an egg; fifty cents for the whole carton of orange juice. I think he even hijacked and tried to resell my parents' coffee in his illicit market. Dad said "No way!" Mom quietly bought an egg. I scoffed. Half an hour later, Peter put everything back in the fridge and went on to play a different game.

My dad bided his time and waited for an opportunity to teach us a lesson about business.

That summer, when my parents had a yard sale, my brothers and I set up a lemonade stand. I also had a side hustle telling jokes from a joke book. (One was "Why does a flamingo stand on one leg? Because if it didn't stand on any it would fall over!") We made a decent amount of money, but I was appalled when my dad told us we needed to pay him for the lemonade and cups we used.

"But we just got them for free from the cupboard!" Peter protested.

"They were not free," Dad retorted. "I had to buy them from the store. And the store had to buy them from the factory. And the factory had to buy the lemons from a farmer."

Mom sidled up next to him and said, "Harlan, maybe we can just let them keep all the money this one time."

"No!" Dad replied, shocked. "I won't have them starting life thinking that productive resources are free!" And so, after a long day selling lemonade, our profit margin was pretty low, except for the money I personally made on jokes. I learned that making a business is costly and there's a risk you won't make enough money for it to be worth it. I also learned that there's a whole chain of buying and selling that goes into a simple cup of lemonade. I began to see why things cost what they cost.

Below are some ways you can enhance your mini-economy experience by having your kids start a business.

What to Do

A mini-economy is, above all, a teaching tool. When children make businesses and participate in a market, it takes the learning to a whole new level—and also the excitement. I might go so far as to say that a mini-economy isn't really complete unless it culminates in a market in which the kids themselves are the sellers. It's actually pretty easy: You just have the kids sell things in your store for both kids and parents to buy.

There are two reasons for this:

- First, creating a business teaches entrepreneurship, which makes them steward their resources for a new goal: investing. In the basic mini-economy, the budget choices they face are giving, saving, and spending. But when they have their own businesses, they can also choose to invest their hard-earned money into their businesses.

- Second, being a part of a market allows kids to see the circular flow of an economy. What does "circular flow" mean? It means that a real economy is not a top-down system. Everyone is both a buyer and a seller, and all of our buying and selling affects everyone else's buying and selling. Every choice affects everyone else. In an economy, we are all truly interconnected.

The Circular Flow of the Economy

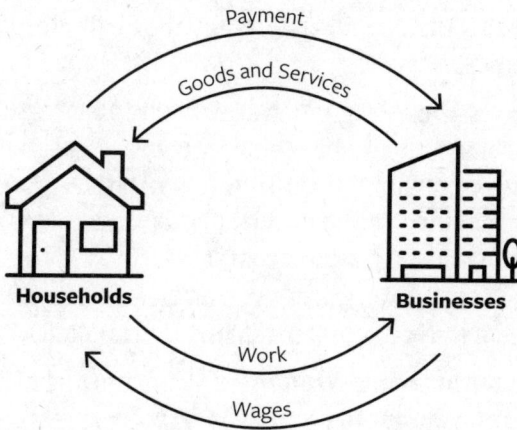

When children shop at other kids' businesses and have others buy from theirs, it puts them in control. Their economic choices are no longer in an environment controlled by adults; the market environment is now running on the choices of the kids in the market. Making a business and operating in a market gives them a new level of autonomy. It also relieves the pressure for parents to purchase things in the (real) store. And frankly, it is more realistic.

There is no one best way for the kids to set up businesses. You should choose what is best for you. I will devote the most time here to discussing how to set up a Big Store Day with other mini-economy families and providing practical resources and steps for making it happen. (See the appendix for how to create a Market Day with many other families or homeschool groups.)

Here are some of the ways to incorporate businesses into your mini-economy:

- **Mini-economy business.** Guide the children to make goods and services that they sell into your store. Store Day looks the same as it does on any other day, except that instead of the adults stocking the whole store, now the kids are supplying things as well. The kids set the prices for their products, though they will probably need guidance.
- **Big Store Day.** Have a market with one or two other families that are also doing a mini-economy. You can have this combined family store at your house. It doesn't take much more planning than a normal playdate and is certainly less planning than a birthday party!
- **Personal business.** Kids can create goods and services that they sell to friends and neighbors for real money.
- **So many more opportunities!** Whether it's helping out at the family business, selling at a farmers' market, or taking part in one of the dozens of entrepreneurship education programs that exist, there are a lot of opportunities out there for kids to get a taste of producing for a real market.

These are all different ways kids can operate in a market. Since each market for a mini-economy business is so different, I'll go through them one at a time. But first, we need to look into what a market is and why it is important for children's learning.

Mini-Economy Businesses

I startled awake on a Saturday morning to a shout of "You're so mean!" Two of my children were locked in verbal combat about the rules of an obscure game they were playing, and their conflict was as ferocious as any that enforces the boundaries of human society and belief. I lurched out of bed to see my four children serried in ranks at the foot of the stairs. As I descended the staircase, the two combatants came to a brief, unspoken truce. A third child was shivering with excitement to show me some art she had already made that morning.

The fourth child was holding a cup of coffee.

I blinked at this incongruous scene. Why did my seven-year-old have coffee? Robbie was more tolerant of grown-up food than his siblings, but this was taking it rather far.

And then I remembered: I'd bought a coupon from him to make the morning coffee!

This business had been my idea (as I wrote earlier, kids often need guidance). I'd told him that it was wonderful to wake up to coffee that's already made, and since he knew how to brew coffee (having scaled the counter and hovered above my shoulder to watch while I was making it), why didn't he welcome us in the morning with fresh-brewed coffee?

He thought this was a great idea, but he set too high a price: 2 DayBucks per day. I told him that was too much. After all, I only earned 3 DayBucks each time I did my job.

"No, it's 2 DayBucks," he insisted.

"Well then, I can't afford it," I replied. "I want to buy from you, but I also want to buy one of Calvin's paper soldiers and Daisy's newspaper, so 2 DayBucks is too much for just one day of coffee." In truth, I thought he'd brew the coffee every day for a week for maybe 5 DayBucks. I suggested a price in this range.

Robbie seemed prepared for negotiation. "OK, 1 DayBuck per day."

"That's still too much!" I protested.

"That's what it is," he said, and I could tell from his nonchalant tone that he was going to stand his ground.

We agreed on 1 DayBuck per day. I paid for two days, and in exchange he handed me two hastily scrawled coffee coupons. I said "Thank you," and he said "Thank you" in reply.

Who do you think won this negotiation? Here's a hint: We both said "Thank you."

We both won. In a trade, both sides gain. That's the point of a market. Robbie got 2 DayBucks that he used for his savings goal. I was handed a hot cup of coffee without even being fully awake, which by happy coincidence helped me navigate the fight between the two other children. (Have you ever been awoken by squabbling children? Wouldn't it be easier if a third child handed you a cup of coffee before you arose to deal with it?)

The mini-economy business is the easiest, most basic way to get your kids involved in entrepreneurship. You just have them make a business at home and sell their products in the household store. You've got a marketplace already set up. Why not add this one extra ingredient? Their parents and siblings are their customers.

Here are some examples from our kids' businesses:

- Twelve-year-old Daisy started a weekly newspaper called the *Dayly News*. It included headlines such as "An Interview with Outsiders" (a.k.a. the neighborhood children), "Saturday Store a Success!," "Sleepover Mania!," and "Four Kingdoms Reduced to Three!" (don't ask). She has also recently written a fan-fiction novel titled *The Calling Woods*, which is based on the Warriors series. It's quite a good book, if I do say so myself.
- Nine-year-old Calvin produced paper and cardboard marvels such as characters from *Star Wars* and *Teenage*

Mutant Ninja Turtles, football players, paper robots, and even a Greek temple.

- Seven-year-old Robbie brewed coffee and then was hired as a worker in Calvin's flourishing paper character business. (Unfortunately, this arrangement didn't work out. "Calvin fired me," Robbie reported.)
- Five-year-old Lucy made drawings, which her parents bought out of charity. Around the holidays, she watered the Christmas tree each morning and plugged the lights in.

Here are some things you'll need to think of when helping kids start their businesses:

- What goods and services should they offer?
- How will they get productive resources (which are not free)?
- What price(s) should they charge?
- How should the adults get the mini-economy money they need too?

Goods and Services

Deciding what goods and services to offer is the fun part! Kids are bursting with creative ideas for things they can sell. If they do need help with business ideas, you can ask them questions like these:

- What is something you enjoy making?
- Is there anything you've made that your friends have been really impressed with?
- Is there anything you've made that makes your friends say "That's so cool!"
- If all your products sell out at Market Day, is there something you could do to help other kids fill the time?

Here's a list of products children have made in real life:

Goods

- Paper robots
- Jewelry
- Bookmarks
- Coffee

Services

- Collecting trash
- Taking an extra job
- Telling jokes
- Braiding hair
- Performing (e.g., singing, poem recital, choreographed dance)
- Giving compliments

Teach the kids that they should find their customers ahead of time before they make their goods and services. This is for two reasons:

- They won't be disappointed if they do a lot of work and then discover no one wants to buy their stuff.
- They'll learn that a business has to satisfy customers' wants. Both sides have to agree to the deal. In a business, customers decide whether to buy or not.

Encourage the kids to sell services as well as goods. Kids love making goods (tangible things) since it's like making art. But having a service to sell in addition to goods means they can stay in business after they've sold out. It also allows them to demonstrate their skills in real time and gives them a new and fun opportunity for interacting with others. For example, it's common for girls to set up hair or nail salons, which are inevitably successful!

Parents will have to decide whether they will allow children to pay other children to do their jobs. I'm not against it in theory. If the work is not family work or service work, then mini-economy job work should be fair game for the market.

The awkward part, of course, would be for a child from another family to be doing a mini-economy job at your house! I think many parents would ban this, and that's OK. On the other hand, my wife was personally very excited about the idea of sending our boys over to pick weeds at their friends' house.

Getting Productive Resources

My dad made his sons pay for cups and lemonade mix when we made our lemonade stand. You should charge the kids for productive resources too. It might seem strange to make them pay for things they can usually use for free, like art supplies. But it's easy to explain to them that it's only fair, since they're selling things made from the supplies back to you. You already had to pay for

SUPPLY AND DEMAND

Robbie told me he didn't have a mini-economy business anymore, after Calvin kicked him out of their paper character making business. I asked him what happened to his coffee making business. He said he was willing to keep doing it if I was willing to pay him 2 Bucks each time he made the coffee. I said that was too expensive, as I would run out of my savings in a week if he made coffee every day, but I'd be willing to pay him if the price were lower. I asked him if it were possible for a business to lower their prices and make more money. He said yes, if they get more customers. But he has still refused to lower his price! He insists on quality.

the supplies at the store. You shouldn't have to pay for them twice. Besides, the kids are making money from their business, and you deserve a cut for the resources you supplied.

As always in the mini-economy, decide these things ahead of time. We set a low price for resources, since we want the kids to make businesses. Art supplies to make several items will only cost 1 DayBuck, unless they use a lot of supplies. There is no rule for setting prices. After all, this is a market, and so there is a lot of freedom to negotiate. Tell the kids it's time to negotiate a price, and find a price that works for everyone.

As I mentioned above, Daisy has written a 150-page novel about talking cats and intends to sell copies of it in our mini-economy and to her friends. I agreed to help with editorial services. Helping her with editing took a lot of time, so I charged her 20 DayBucks. That's a lot of money, but I'll be buying books from her as well. It might seem silly that I would charge her for helping her make the book, but she will be paid for copies of the book. This perfectly illustrates how a real economy works. Money flows between producers and consumers and back again. The process helps us specialize, be more productive, and get the goods and services we want. The kids understand this when they see it work in a mini-economy.

Congratulations! Your kids are starting to get a deep understanding of how a supply chain works. They're learning that the things we buy don't just appear on the store shelves. It takes the hard work of an entrepreneur to get them there.

Setting Prices

Explain to the kids that they need to think carefully about what price to charge. They should set a price that reflects both the cost of their work (resources plus their time) and what customers are willing to pay. Remind them no one is forced to buy their stuff. They have to make their customers happy. They can also change prices later if they want to sell more things.

Kids will often set prices too low. They are focused on selling as much stuff as they can. Ask them to consider what will make them more money: selling more things at a lower price or fewer things at a higher price.

Your kids are discovering that prices aren't arbitrary. They are learning that prices reflect the needs of both buyers and sellers, giving them even more insight into how money works.

Adults in the Mini-Economy

As I discussed earlier in the book, it's good for adults to have mini-economy jobs too. It creates the opportunity for the whole family to be doing jobs at the same time, and it shows that parents are willing to do what they're asking children to do. We also see that it creates the chance for a more robust marketplace. If adults earn Bucks, they can spend them on Store Day. This means you can include things in the store only grown-ups would want, as well as some things that both adults and kids will want. For example, parents will probably be happy to buy stories the kids wrote or pay to see their performances.

In a Big Store, children are able to sell to a slightly larger market. This is exciting for them, and it also challenges them to create something people actually want, not just a cute thing for Mom or Dad. When the kids are planning what to make for their businesses, parents should challenge them: "Now remember, you need to think of things the other family will want, both the parents and the kids." This will stretch their entrepreneurial muscles a bit more.

Big Store Day

Big Store Day is perfect for if you know at least one other family that is also doing a mini-economy. Selling to "outsiders" (as Daisy's newspaper called her neighbor friends) cranks up the excitement level and makes the kids grapple with the circular flow of the economy—because everyone is both a buyer and a seller.

You'll need a couple ingredients to have a successful Big Store Day at your house:

- Two or three families participating in a mini-economy.
- Agreement between parents on prices and the value of the money.

Let's go through each point to see why they are important, what you need to do, and why they are totally feasible.

Two or Three Families

A three-family Big Store Day brings the children a rich enough business experience while being easy to implement. It's a lot like having family friends over for coffee and a playdate but with an activity in which both adults and kids take part.

What if there are no other partnering mini-economy families available? Can your children just sell items in your normal family store? Sure, and that might work for you. But there's not many shoppers, so the parents would probably end up buying the kids' items, assuming their siblings don't. That's not too bad, but for me it's a bit too contrived.

On the other hand, if there are three families involved, the store might have twelve or more shoppers (assuming two parents and two kids per family), with all parents and kids both buying and selling at the store. It becomes more likely that someone will buy the children's products. If no one does, then parents can buy them as a backup option.

You can certainly have more than a couple families involved, but then it becomes a larger Market Day and the logistic load increases. I want to keep things easy on you!

Agreement on Prices and the Value of Money

If a family you're inviting over doesn't have their own mini-economy, you can just give them some Bucks to spend at your store. If the other family does have a mini-economy, talk with the parents about how much money their kids have earned over the summer. If both sets of kids have about the same amount of money, they can both use household currencies at the Big Store.

If another family has significantly different amounts of money, then that creates a problem. The family with more money will be able to buy more stuff. You might have to set up an exchange rate between families or even create a new money system. (In this case, see the appendix.)

- - - -

Businesses really complete a mini-economy. Kids need practice with money. When they have businesses, they are making many more choices about money. Not just choices about saving and spending but also choices about controlling costs, setting prices, making products, gaining new skills, and standing up for oneself in negotiations. They learn how to say "No deal!" and find new solutions. Running a business teaches kids they can master every aspect of handling money.

Things to Add to Your Mini-Economy

- Kid businesses are the best part of a mini-economy. They teach kids about money on a whole new level.
- Adults should save their Bucks to spend on the goods and services from kids' businesses.
- Talk with the kids about what they should charge for their products. Remind them that they're the boss! If they charge too little, they won't make much money. But if they charge too much, others won't be able to afford their products.

- Charge kids for resources. If they are using household art or cleaning supplies, for example, they should pay a little for these. Decide ahead of time what the cost will be.
- Remember that when kids have businesses, they have the power to negotiate. They can and should use it.
- Empower them!

—— THINK and TEACH ——

Questions for Parents

1. What beliefs do you have about making a business? Is it something you think you can do? Or does it seem like something other people would do?
2. Are children's businesses something you are comfortable introducing early in the mini-economy? Why or why not?
3. Are you personally more risk-averse? Or are you more risk-tolerant?
4. Which of your children do you think are more risk-averse? More risk-tolerant?

Questions for Children

1. What is something new you've created that you are proud of?
2. What will happen if your business makes a good or service that no one wants?
3. When is a time you've had to take a risk? Was the risk worth it?
4. Why is making a business risky?
5. How is shopping at the mini-economy store different from buying something from a family member's business?

6. What does it mean to "be your own boss" when you make a business?

7. Which is better, charging a lower price for your product or a higher price? What are the good things and bad things about each choice?

Lessons for Children

1. When you make your own business, you get to be your own boss.

2. A business provides goods and services that people want.

3. If you see problems, you can think of ways to fix them and get paid for doing it.

4. Starting a business brings risk. You have to spend money and time to run your business. This time and money could be used for other things.

5. When you make a business, you have to be polite to your customers.

6. When you make a business, no one tells you what the right answers are. You have to decide for yourself.

PART 3

TYING IT ALL TOGETHER

Great job starting your mini-economy! How's it going? A few things might have tripped you up along the way, and you may also be getting new ideas for what to do next. Our family experienced both of these as we went on our mini-economy journey.

For example, I was getting frustrated that the kids never bought a coupon for a family doughnut trip. Saturday after Saturday, I hoped that one of them would pipe up and say, "Dad! How much is a family doughnut trip, again?" I planned to benevolently say "Just two DayBucks each," and then lead them all to Country Style Doughnuts for a wonderful family memory.

Instead, it was me asking them, "Kids, doesn't anyone want to buy a doughnut trip?" This was greeted with shrugs. After a couple weeks of this I gave up—and took them out for Saturday doughnuts anyway. As I drove down the road, I swore I could hear them sniggering in the backseat. "We knew Dad wanted doughnuts most of all, so if we just waited long enough, we wouldn't have to pay for them." (Did they actually say this, or was it just the guilt in my head talking? Anyway, it was true.)

I had made a mistake: I put something in the store that I wanted them to have—OK, let's be honest, that I wanted me to have. All they had to do was wait me out, and I caved.

This might not seem so bad, but it's really important. If we make them pay for things they're likely to get anyway, it devalues the store, which has the chain reaction of devaluing their play money and even their jobs because everything in the little economy is interconnected. This is something we must get right.

⬛ ⬛ ⬛ ⬛

I confess, I was hesitant to write this book because I knew I wasn't the first person to come up with the idea of a home economy. My own parents used one, and I'm sure many other parents have too. What gives me the right to write? The thing is, that's exactly the reason: I knew that parents everywhere would be putting together little economies, and they're likely to make the same mistakes I did. By sharing the mistakes the Day family has made, maybe I can help others avoid them.

In these last few chapters, we'll talk about mistakes and about those what-ifs that pop up. And finally, we'll tackle one big question: What happens when the kids age out of the elementary school years? How can we help them take their next steps in gaining financial capability as they approach the teen years?

10

Mistakes

Remember, a mini-economy is a structure for helping kids make choices about money over time. The most common mistakes that parents make end up undermining that structure, hampering choice, or snarling up the consistent timing of work and rewards. A mini-economy doesn't have to be complicated. In fact, it is sometimes best when it's really simple. But it must be consistent.

In this chapter, we'll go over a few bumps on the road I've encountered in our house and learned from both other parents and classroom teachers who have done mini-economies over the years. You can see that they are not too difficult to avoid and that it doesn't take too much to get a mini-economy running smoothly.

Learning about these mistakes also shows you principles for teaching kids about money in other circumstances. Let's work through the following common mistakes so you can learn how to avoid messing this up:

- Putting things in the store they don't want or will get anyway.
- Replacing family rules with mini-economy payments and fines.

- Making your mini-economy all about controlling the kids' behavior.
- Giving too many fines.
- Allowing debt.
- Saying "Will you do it if I pay you for it?"
- Telling kids to do something while they are watching TV (or other devices).
- Setting store prices too low.
- Setting store prices too high.
- Making impulse buys.

Sell Things They Want

I covered this a few times already, so I won't dwell on it here. But this is the mistake that most bedeviled our own mini-economy, so I want to reiterate it.

Decide what to put in the store by making a list of things that the kids bug you for, such as toys they pick up in the toy aisle at Target and privileges they agitate for. Believe it or not, it's even helpful to sell things that are slightly bad for them, like sugar or screen time. Why? Because you want to give them the truly wholesome things for free. You don't want to put yourself in a situation in which you feel like you have to withhold something you think your kids need because you've made a coupon for it.

Like I mentioned earlier, the best coupons to put in the store are for things you sometimes say yes but usually say no to. Use the store to ration these things. Related: Plan to refresh your store. In our store, the things that didn't get bought kind of just stayed there. Daisy even mumbled one time "Same old store." When you buy things for the store, don't put them all out in the first week. Keep some items back so you can regularly introduce something new. This will keep the excitement going, which in turn maintains the value of the money and hence the value of their jobs.

Don't Replace Family Rules

House rules are still rules. Children should not be able to buy their way out of obeying the rules. In *The Classroom Mini-Economy*, Harlan Day recommends that teachers not start their mini-economy until October. Why wait? Because it's important to get the classroom rules and expectations firmly established before adding an economic system.

Even in real life, the economic system does not replace the legal system. On the contrary, the economic system rests upon and relies upon the legal system.

Don't Make It About Controlling Behavior

It's great if your mini-economy helps your children behave. However, this can't be the main reason for it. Remember, it is a structure for making choices about work and money over time. This allows them to face the outcomes of their choices and to reap the benefits of their increased productivity. It's not mainly about rewarding them for following the rules.

The mini-economy is one tool of many you can use to motivate your children to productive action, as well as to incentivize them to be helpful. A well-working mini-economy lets them demonstrate and build competence in their tasks and gives them a chance to practice exercising autonomy. It cannot be a primary method of behavior management. But if their behavior improves as a result—and it might—that's a great outcome.

Don't Give Too Many Fines

It's OK to charge the kids fines, but only for certain specific behaviors that the kids know about ahead of time. If you get angry and randomly charge them money for misbehaving, you will quickly lose their buy-in to the mini-economy. It will lose its power. It will seem to the children like a new and sneaky way for the grown-ups to keep them under control. A mini-economy is supposed to be a structure in which kids can make choices about work and money over time, not a set of rewards and punishments.

A good way to levy fines is as a natural consequence of a child's actions. An example of this comes from Lauren, a kindergarten teacher who runs a classroom mini-economy. In her mini-economy, if students lose their pencils and don't have anything to write with, they can always buy one from the classroom store. This may function like a fine, but in reality it is an obvious natural consequence of losing a pencil, not a punishment. You need a pencil? Here's one for sale. At home, a parent could sell or loan kids items that they lose for a fee.

Just remember these two rules if you are using fines:

- Don't use fines too much.
- Kids should understand what actions are finable ahead of time so that they can plan their actions. Avoiding fines is one way out of many that kids can make choices about money over time, which is the goal.

Say No to Debt

When you buy something using debt, there's nothing in the future to work toward except getting out of debt. It's really hard to motivate the kids to work toward a goal if that goal is simply paying off something they already own.

In the section on taxes, I discussed how Sarah and I let the kids get a trampoline at the beginning of the summer, so they could use it all season, and pay it off throughout the summer with taxes. We did make them save up for a certain amount as a down payment first. They voted for a high tax rate so they could get the down payment quickly. (And Daisy donated her own money. She really wanted that trampoline.)

This really messed up our mini-economy for several weeks. It made the kids not want to work. Not only were the taxes high but they didn't have anything to work toward. In fact, when they almost refused to do their jobs, I told them that I was going to "repo" the trampoline and not let them use it while their payments were in default! Shocked, they got back to work.

I learned something about debt through this experience. Not only does debt burden you over time, it also leaves you with nothing to aspire to. You've already gotten your reward; now there's nothing left but to labor to pay it back. How much better to have a goal to work toward! Saving is better.

This episode taught the kids a few things about debt. And I learned my lesson too: I won't repeat the mistake of selling items on credit. We just need to plan ahead better next time.

Don't Say "Will You Do It If I Pay You for It?"

The fastest way to ruin your mini-economy is to start randomly bribing kids to do things. Work should be decided upon ahead of time, almost like a contract.

Bribing kids to do random tasks, to do what parents command, or to behave undermines the ethos of your economy. It also undermines parental authority and cheapens the rules. It weakens the structure you've already set in place in your house.

Parents need to set expectations ahead of time for the work kids do around the house. Assigning work randomly can cause drama. Define and be consistent about the tasks kids are paid for and the ones they must complete for no pay.

If your kids ask you to pay them for something new, don't do it right away. Stop and consider. Talk with your spouse. Talk with the children and ask why they think they should be paid. Don't do it right then; wait a week. This will give you time to find out if it's a good idea and if it fits in the rules of your house. Sometimes you should go ahead and let them take on new tasks. In this case, they deserve a raise.

Save Your Breath

It is a waste of time and energy to tell kids to do something while they are watching TV (or other devices). Telling kids to do something while they are engrossed in a screen never works. Press pause, then talk to them. Better yet, make sure they know what they are expected to do before the TV ever comes on.

Don't Set Prices Too Low

Oops. Your children are better workers than you thought they would be. They are taking on extra jobs, you are paying them extra, and they are buying up gobs of candy, screen time, and stay-up-late time. This is getting out of control! What should you do?

First, resist the urge to simply raise prices. This will seem like a bait-and-switch—and it is. You will lose the kids' buy-in to the mini-economy if they suspect you might change the rules on them at any time.

You do have a couple of options. The first is to let it happen. Remember, a mini-economy gives them access to *treats*. It will go on break from time to time (maybe for the entire school year). So these treats will not last their entire childhood. You can loudly lament that your kids have tricked you by working hard and getting more things from the store than you thought they would. They will love this, and they will be proud of themselves and their hard work. That's a win. It might violate your normal rules, but there are guardrails in place so that it doesn't go on like this forever.

If things really are out of control, you can simply let things in the store sell out. For example, if stay-up-late coupons are causing fights, then let the coupons run out. Don't restock them. Introduce new items and coupons at higher prices, and tell the kids that the cheap stay-up-late coupons were nice while they lasted.

Don't Set Prices Too High

On the other hand, making store prices too high will freeze the store since the kids simply won't buy the expensive things in it. If you think you've set prices too high, it's best to encourage the kids to save their money for later. You can put some of the items on sale at next week's store. Don't put them on sale right then and there. It will make you look desperate.

Resist Impulse Buys

This mistake is about real stores, not your household store. We have a family rule that you have to want something before you go into a store if you are going to buy it. You can't decide you want something while you're in the store and buy it then.

Now, that might sound overly restrictive. Why not just let the kids spend their own money? First of all, this is a rule for adults too, not just kids. We call it the "Before the Store" rule, and it's a wise lifelong habit for everyone's personal finances. You'll be amazed at how a store can convince you that you "need" something you didn't know you needed! Giving yourself and the kids a little space from the urgency of the products in the store can help everyone make calmer, more rational spending choices.

Kids get this. As my daughter Daisy put it, "If we just buy whatever we want, the house would get too crowded."

Second, children are even more impulsive than adults. The Before the Store rule helps you help them not blow all their money. It instills solid financial habits. And it will even help you with your grown-up finances.

—— THINK and TEACH ——

Questions for Parents

1. Which of these common mistakes have you made?
2. Do you disagree with any of these "mistakes"? Are there any that you feel are not really mistakes?

Questions for Children

1. Do you think that paying a fine is a fair punishment if you break a rule? Would it be better or worse than a timeout?
2. Why do you think we have the rule that you have to plan ahead to buy something before we go in the store?
3. If a kid loses a toy, should the parents buy them a new one? Or should they pay the whole cost themselves?

Lessons for Children

1. We don't just do chores for money. We also do them to help the family.
2. There are some jobs that we all do together.
3. We don't buy things the first time we see them.
4. We have to know we want something before we go in the store if we are going to buy it.

11

What If?

In your mini-economy, surprises will pop up. This chapter will help you avoid some of them and perhaps also help you think of any more snags your kids might hit before they can happen.

What If a Child Says, "This Is All Just a Trick to Get the Kids to Do More Work"?

In fact, my son Robbie said exactly that. We had just rebooted our mini-economy for the fourth summer. I had an answer prepared: "But this way you get more stuff than you would have. And we would have made you do chores anyway. If we weren't doing mini-economy, you'd still have to do chores; you just wouldn't get paid for them."

What If Something Unexpected Happens?

Plan to be flexible. Emphasis on the "plan" part. When something pops up that you didn't expect, try to adhere to your original plan as much as you can in that particular incident. But then make a new plan for next time. You can do this by talking through your mini-economy practices with your children. Involving them in discussions about managing work, money, and responsibilities over time is one of the best ways to teach them.

What If a Child Wants to Pay Another Child to Do Their Job?

This should be OK, but only because mini-economy jobs are extra, on top of *family work*. You should not allow children to pay their way out of basic responsibilities. But trading money for work is acceptable in an economy, including a mini-economy.

As a rule of thumb, if a child's job has a *title*, like Gardener or Librarian, then it's a job they can pay a sibling to do. But don't allow them to just shell out money to pay for casually wrecking a public space.

One mini-economy parent, Taylor, reported that this actually worked pretty well in her house. "Our second born (age four) loved being able to pay her older sister to not have to do her chores!" Since the older sister was happy to do the chores for extra money, they both got what they wanted. But the older sister was able to buy more things on Store Day—a valuable lesson for all of the kids.

What If a Child Asks for More Jobs?

If a child wants more work, go ahead and let them do more jobs. And yes, pay them in full. Remember that a mini-economy is a way to help children grow. It's not a constraint. Your child is asking you if they can work harder in order to strive more toward their goals. That's something you want to encourage.

Maybe you're concerned that this child will be able to buy too many things or their siblings will find it unfair. But think about it: Your child is *asking if they can do more housework*. That's a big win! Would they have done that without a mini-economy in place? Letting them do another job teaches them (and you) that they really are capable of more focus and ambition than you had originally thought. It also shows them that there is important work to be done all around us and teaches them to be observant and find what that work is. And it demonstrates that they can achieve goals quickly if they engage in some focused effort.

Their higher earning power might overwhelm your family store, and they might be able to easily buy lots of things that you thought were going to be more difficult to obtain. For example, your child might use extra jobs to buy extra candy. Are you slightly horrified at the amount of sugar you're allowing them to consume? Yes. But you should think of this as a win. Remember that these lessons about money will last a lifetime. A few extra grams of sugar now can prevent ruinous debt in the future. Besides, with no mini-economy, they would have asked and asked for the candy, and you would have given them some arbitrary amount. It wouldn't have taught them any lesson—except perhaps that the more they ask, the more they are likely to get. The hassle would have been all on you. Now, you can see how valuable this is to your kid. They are willing to put in the work.

Is it fair for the other children? Yes. The work one child does will not take anything away from the others. A mini-economy job is productive. That means your hard-working child is creating new value where it otherwise would not have existed. The family gets to enjoy the benefits of the extra work too. Let's say that the new job is to pick up the toys and pine cones from the yard. The children now don't have to worry about stepping on the prickly cones, and it's quicker and easier to mow the lawn.

Remind the other children that they are welcome to do more jobs also. Say it sincerely. It's just a choice that is open. Don't chide them for laziness or use their eager sibling as an example of a model child. You can just tell them, "Having more printouts is really important to your sibling, so they are willing to do more work to get them. That's their choice. It doesn't take anything from you. It makes the house nicer for all of us. It brings more money for giving and taxes. They are paying the price to reach their goal."

Another option is for a child to start a household business doing extra work. The child can negotiate payment, but in this case the payment comes from parents or siblings, the people who are directly benefiting from the work. (See chapter 9 for more details on household businesses.)

What If My Child Refuses to Do Their Job?

In this instance, it matters whether this is an isolated or ongoing case. If it's isolated, it is not a big deal. It's just a choice. In some cases it's OK to just let the child know that some weeks are difficult and that they can take the week off—but they won't be paid. However, I think you should avoid this approach if you can, for the reasons I outline in the chapters on motivation and working. For the most part, kids should be doing their jobs.

Here are some things you can try.

First, try to head this off before it happens. There are several things you can do at the very beginning of the mini-economy, including building the store with the whole family's input, which is very important. You will have already scouted out things your children really want.

Second, if your children are able to pick jobs from a list of suggestions and even to suggest work of their own, then they are more likely to be interested in the work.

Third, you can have an honest conversation with your child about what's wrong. You might find something to change. Giving your child a voice in how the mini-economy is run increases buy-in and helps them think through how the system works—a valuable lesson.

Fourth, having the store right after the kids do their jobs and get paid makes a tight connection between the work they do and the things they can buy. Getting to participate in the store is usually a powerful incentive to work.

Fifth, make sure your child understands the implications of the choice not to work. Be specific: "You said you wanted to go with Dad to the Kickers game. You can buy that privilege with Bucks." Your child will be reminded of the value of their work and the things they want to buy.

And finally, I suggest reviewing chapter 4, which is about motivation and will give you the guidelines you need.

Remember, I recommend that you divide work into different categories. Family work and service work are things that must be done for no pay. (Use the guidelines in chapter 5 to help your child understand the value of this work and why they must do it.)

In principle, jobs that kids get paid for fall into the category of "extra jobs they don't have to do." If you aren't running a mini-economy at the moment, I think it's OK to let them choose whether to do extra jobs or not. But it doesn't make for a very interesting mini-economy if some of the kids just aren't participating. If you're doing a mini-economy, it's best to get their buy-in ahead of time and then make the kids do the work even when they don't feel like it.

One parent, Oleg, explained their family's mini-economy like this: "I have two kids in my house. The one decided to have a high level of consumption, and so he works a lot. He makes a lot of money and buys things that he wants. The second kid doesn't like work. But she also doesn't care about buying things. As a result, she doesn't work at all. She doesn't buy anything, but it's a valid choice." Though this is worrying, it is far better that the daughter learns the connection between work and consumption than if her parents simply bought her things regardless of whether she worked hard or not. She has made her clear-eyed choice, and she seems content to live with it.

A mini-economy is a great system, but it is not the be-all and end-all of parenting. You can let it run its course, allow the other children to enjoy it, and then move to something different. But you'll need a different system for teaching your kids about money and work.

What If This Is Too Abstract for My Child?

Maybe your child has a short attention span or craves instant gratification. It seems far-fetched that they could commit to all of this waiting. But hold on: That describes most children!

Mini-economies are used in elementary classrooms all around the world. We know they work, at least for most children. They are designed for small children. The weekly store is not too far in the future, and the monetary payments for doing work provide an instant reward of sorts. Trust me, kids love getting paid. It makes them feel grown-up. And a large part of why we're doing this in the first place is to stretch kids' attention spans a bit. The mini-economy is a system in which they can grow.

We had this issue with my younger daughter when she was four. In addition to her job as Zookeeper, she got paid 1 Buck for using the big potty instead of the little training potty. (We called the training potty the Penguin Potty. And yes, I thought she was too old for it. That was the point of trying to get her to stop using it.) But going potty in the most convenient way was more important to her than getting paid extra. So at first she passed up many opportunities to make money. I nearly just confiscated the Penguin Potty, but I wanted to give her the chance to earn some money by delaying gratification. After a couple of weeks, she started using the Penguin Potty a bit less. She was very proud and excited to get extra money—it helped her catch up to her siblings' savings. At that point it was a bit easier to take away the little potty, so we did.

There are some things you can do for the especially impatient child. One idea from a parent, Ella, is to put smaller boundaries around the work the child does. So rather than having the child range around the house picking up stuffed animals (as in the Zookeeper's job), the job can be to clean a smaller area. That is, give the child responsibility over a clear, distinct area that is easy to picture.

Another idea is to help the child visualize the rewards for which they are working. Here are a few ways to do this:

- Keep the store fresh. For example, add one or two new things to the store each week.
- Don't let the child forget what rewards await in the store. Show the store items, including the new items, to your kids at the beginning of the week to remind them of their shopping goals.
- Allow the option of buying a mini-privilege—for example, a nice snack—with the newly earned money right after the child completes their work. This can help immediately connect the work to the reward. Of course, give them the option to save that money too.

Remember, some kids would always rather get immediate gratification. That's not necessarily a bad outcome. Sure, we would rather the mini-economy teach them to become a big saver. But maybe this is a first step for them in learning delayed gratification. It gives them a context for thinking about getting something now versus getting it later. And sometimes, they suddenly come around!

—— THINK AND TEACH ——

Questions for Parents

1. Which of your children is likely to take on an extra job?
2. How can you set up boundaries for your kids' work to make it easier to understand?
3. Is your child going to struggle with a mini-economy being too abstract? How can you simplify other parts of the mini-economy to make it easier for kids to understand?

Questions for Children

1. What is some work you've done that you enjoyed? Have you made anything that you liked making?
2. What job would you like to do when you grow up? (Parents: Take that answer and create a household job to match it.)

Lessons for Children

1. We all need to help out at home.
2. Living in a nice home takes work.
3. We can't get all the things we want, but we can get some of them.
4. We can get more things by either working more or saving more.

12

What Comes Next

My daughter Daisy has been a part of our mini-economy for five years, and I'm wondering if she's aging out of it. For the first few years, we did mini-economy only during the summer, but this last year we have continued throughout the school year.

She has grown in her knowledge and habits with work and money. When we first introduced the household store, I asked the kids how they planned to spend their money (after they had given their 10 percent donation). In the first summer, eight-year-old Daisy replied, "I want to make a pattern. So one week I will buy something small, like one piece of candy. The next week I'll buy something big. Small, big, small, big."

It was a moment for me to wonder at the wonderful mind of a child! My mind is practical and budget focused. Daisy's is more imaginative. But inside the framework of a values-based plan, Daisy had freedom to think through how she wanted to manage money. I still don't know if making a spending pattern has a practical value, but it got her thinking about how to use money. It helped teach her that she has control over her money. Kids need to practice making meaningful choices about money over time, and she took advantage.

Two years later, she had a different approach. She wanted to buy a hoverboard. You know, the two-wheeled gyroscope-balanced electric vehicles. (I think *hoverboard* is a tragic misnomer. The boards do not actually hover, unlike the ones from *Back to the Future Part II*). I told her that since it was expensive, she'd probably have to save up all summer for it.

She told me, "I think I can get it faster." She proceeded to pull together all the resources at her disposal to expedite the achievement of her goal. (Recall that DayBucks can be exchanged for US dollars at a rate of two-to-one.) She used birthday money, took an extra job, had DayBucks saved up from the previous summer that I didn't know about, and even—appallingly—asked a friend who gave her a birthday present if she could return that gift for store credit and use it to buy the hoverboard. It wasn't classy, but she achieved her goal quickly. Thus she was able to buy the contraption two short weeks after I told her it would take all summer.

She had demonstrated that she could be ruthlessly goal oriented with money. And borderline rude, if you count the returning of the birthday present. But she was certainly not lacking in initiative and gumption.

When Daisy was twelve, her goal orientation reached a new level. We had begun amassing tax money to buy our big trampoline, which I told the kids they could buy on credit once they had enough for a down payment. At this point, Daisy was too old to be interested in many of the items in our store, but she was really excited about the trampoline. She volunteered to donate all her money to the down payment and encouraged her siblings to do the same. They didn't want to since they had other saving goals. But for Daisy, it didn't matter that her siblings weren't donating much. She wanted the trampoline and she wanted it soon. She donated her entire salary and savings for the next two weeks, and the kids quickly amassed enough for the down payment.

You learn a lot about your children when you watch how they manage money. She displayed grace, generosity, and leadership. She also showed verve and quick decision-making when she saw something worth getting. She identified what it would cost her and wasted no time paying that cost and reaching her goal.

But what's this about her being "too old to be interested in many of the items in our store"? She is above the age that I recommend for mini-economy and is reaching her adolescent years. What's next?

My wife, Sarah, had wise words: "Daisy should still be part of the economy because she's part of the family. We're a team." After all, the parents are part of the mini-economy too. We have jobs and spend money on the kids' businesses. Why shouldn't older kids remain involved?

What to Do Next

A mini-economy transitions easily to the real economy if you have an exchange rate between mini-economy money and real money, such as 2 DayBucks to 1 US dollar. As the kids get older, I notice more and more instances in which they'd prefer to take the real money.

Older children will also get wise to your plan if you've been making some items more expensive in your store and some cheaper. For example, we sell coupons for treats from the concession stand at the pool or the ice cream truck that comes by the soccer field. I don't like letting them get this because it causes the other kids to get jealous, so our coupons actually make the treats more expensive in DayBucks than in dollars. (For example, a treat that costs 6 DayBucks might only cost $3 in real money.) However, the older children do the math and use whichever currency gets them a better deal. I'm fine with this. It means they know what they're doing.

You don't need to get rid of the mini-economy money and pay them directly in dollars, though. Older children still value coupons for privileges, and privilege coupons remain a good way to regulate their use. Daisy is still willing to pay for candy and screen time. By the time she's sixteen, she will probably even be willing to buy coupons to use my car! But I'm not there yet, so I'm open to ideas.

The teen years are a great time for kids to grow in autonomy over money choices. Teens should earn money with the classic teen jobs: babysitting, lawn-mowing, pet-sitting, and, as they get older, jobs that require and build more skill such as lifeguarding, restaurant work, office work, construction, and other jobs in the real economy. They should have some freedom to spend money on things they want. They should have goals. But parents should emphasize that the budgeting principles learned in the mini-economy still hold: When they get a paycheck, they should first donate a portion and then save a portion. Continued guidance from parents may not sound like autonomy. But it is *teaching*. When you help them take their mini-economy habits and consciously apply them to their teen job, they are continuing the growth trajectory you've been teaching them since they were small children. You are supporting their growth and maturity by connecting their early-life lessons to their adolescent experiences.

Planning for Education After High School

Today's economy is based on skill. Sure, teenagers can walk into a restaurant with no skills, get a job, and still make money. They just have to be able to show up on time and be willing to learn. But such low expectations don't last long. If anyone wants to make more money, they need to acquire more skills. This comes partly from experience in the job and partly from education. "Education" after high school usually means college. Not everyone needs to go to college, but everyone should have a plan to gain more skills if they want their earnings to increase much over time.

Before 2010, there was one overriding message about college: Everyone should go. Since then, societal attitudes about college have become more complicated. People are skeptical about the value of a traditional college education, and there is renewed interest in career-focused training. At the same time, many families prepare for college as if it were the Hunger Games. Parents have their children preparing years in advance to produce glowing college applications, along with test preparation classes, loads of extracurricular activities, Advanced Placement classes, and (for top college applications) founding a club or nonprofit. The rat race begins at age thirteen—maybe earlier.

If your teens have practice making meaningful, values-based choices about money and work over time, then they are well-prepared to face this environment. If they can manage money, know their skills, and know (generally) the kind of life they want to live, they can plan more easily for life after high school.

Consider the following choices a young person needs to make about education:

- What kind of school should I attend?
- What should my major be?
- Why do I want to go back to school? (What are my values?)
  - To make more money?
  - To prepare for a career?
  - To have fun?
  - To learn for its own sake?
  - Because that's just what people do?
  - Because my parents went to school there?
- Should I take out student loans?
- Should I have a job while I'm in school?
- Can I graduate on time?
- What kind of job will I need to support my lifestyle?
- What kind of lifestyle and job will I need to pay back college loans quickly?

Notice that none of these questions are "Can I get into the best college?" Yes, degrees from more prestigious colleges are associated with more prestigious jobs. Teens that have the ability to succeed at a top college should consider trying to get accepted. But the answer might not be college at all. Not everyone needs to go to college. However, everyone needs a plan for getting some kind of educational certification after high school, whether it's an associate's degree, a certification, military experience, or something else. Today's economy runs on skill, and everyone should have a plan to upgrade their skills and have something to show for it.

I'm not so concerned about how good of a college (by which I mean a place to get some educational certification after high school, not necessarily a four-year degree) my kids go to as much as I am concerned about how successful they will be once they get there—and after they graduate.

What are some bad outcomes? There are many possibilities:

- Teen years that are all stress, doing activities the teen doesn't like.
- Not graduating from college on time, leading to unnecessary costs.
- Attending a college that costs more than necessary; the student could get just as good an education elsewhere for a lower price.
- Needing to take a high-paying but disliked job after college just to pay the loans back.
- Not paying student loans back fast enough, leading to years of debt.

How can young people avoid these outcomes? By talking with parents and thinking ahead about their goals. If a teen wants to aim high, they should do it! But they must also be realistic about what the impact of college costs will be after graduation. Weigh the costs against the benefits and the risks against the possibilities.

A successful education is one that is planned for. You know this already because all successful financial decisions are planned for! That's why a mini-economy is for teaching kids how to make meaningful choices about money and work over time. When a teen plans for college using the tools learned in a childhood mini-economy, they will be able to get good outcomes that are the opposite of the bad ones listed above, such as:

- Middle and high school years that are busy with enjoyable activities that build the teen up.
- Graduating on time.
- Finding an education that is worth the price.
- Getting a job that they want, or at least being on track to get the job they want (sometimes these things take time).
- No loans, or loans that are low enough that they can be quickly paid off.
- Understanding loans and the importance of paying off loans quickly.

How can you get started? By talking with your teen about the questions above. You can also begin saving for college. Not only does this mean that there is money available for college, but knowing there is money saved makes kids more motivated to go to college. Talking with them about college saving will also help motivate you, the parent, to find ways to save. Furthermore, talking with your teen about it will help them envision what comes next and understand the value of their teenage activities. It will also help them attach values to their habits—exactly what you've been training them to do in your mini-economy.

College savings should be in some kind of investment account, often a 529 fund. Here are a few practical things you can do for engaging your child's interest in saving and investment:

1. Have a 529 account.
2. Buy the kids a stock that starts with the letter A, then for each birthday, get them a stock that starts with the next letter of the alphabet. (This is an idea from Grandma Sue Beckman.)
3. Allow the kids to buy real-world stocks or mutual funds using the mini-economy exchange rate (in my family's case, 2 DayBucks for every US dollar.) They can pitch in with parents to buy such an investment. You can track the performance of your shared investment together. It's a great way to continue to teach a kid to save.
4. Allow them to invest in each other's mini-economy businesses.
5. Give the kids a raise for attending school successfully.
6. Above all, *talk* with your children about how to pay for college. This might be difficult and embarrassing for parents, but it is so valuable.

—— THINK AND TEACH ——

Questions for Parents

1. What were your experiences with work as a teen? Did you have a job? What did your parents expect?
2. What expectations do you have for teenagers' work?
3. What do you think the value of education is?
4. What expectations do you have for your children's education?
5. Do you have money saved for college?

Questions for Children

1. What job do you want when you grow up?
2. What kind of work do you like to do?
3. What have you created that made you feel successful?
4. How important is it to you to earn lots of money? Why?
5. What kind of job would you be willing to do for less money?

Lessons for Children

1. People's pay is determined by their skills. (This might not be true for every person at every moment, but it is true on average and over time.)
2. People gain skill both by working and by getting further education.

3. You need to plan for education just like you plan what to do with money.

4. College brings lots of benefits: It helps you get a better job, it's fun, it allows you to meet new people, and it expands your horizon. But each of those things comes with a cost, so it's important to decide what each benefit is worth to you.

AFTERWORD

"This was an *awesome* day," Robbie declared.

What made the day awesome? In between Robbie's basketball game, going to a sword store (yes, real swords), and watching *The Lord of the Rings: The Two Towers*, the kids had to do double chores.

How could double chores be part of an awesome day?

If you set up the chores well, there are times when the kids will love them. In this case, we had to remove some bushes to make way for a shed and take care of a large branch that had fallen on our trampoline and damaged it. We teamed up to dig out the bushes with shovels, and when we found the roots tangled together, we hacked them with the hatchet. Then we cut up the fallen branch. We worked together, learned about roots, built skill, and learned to use interesting tools (under supervision). We also arranged the chores so they maximized motivation, like I discussed in chapter 4.

When we finished and went inside, everyone got paid. The kids knew what to do. They put money in the donation box and the tax box. We discussed the implications of the tragic destruction of our trampoline, which they had paid for using tax money. We decided that the kids would pay for part of a replacement through renewed taxation and the parents would cover the rest.

Then we opened the store.

"I need to save my money to buy copies of my book," said Daisy, referring to the printing of the novel she wrote.

"I saved up 200 DayBucks!" rejoiced Calvin, who had been trying to set a saving record.

"I want to buy that wallet and buy US dollars so I can get a hat at the Bass Pro Shop," said Robbie.

"I want to buy that stuffie," said Lucy, who always buys stuffies.

Each kid learned from the others' saving and spending practices, and each one was proud of the work they'd done that day. They deserved their pay.

I was struck by how fluent they were in talking about money. I didn't agree with all their money choices, but I had a context to discuss their choices with them. They were able to communicate their plans in detail and with confidence. It's not just because I've taught them about money. It's because they've had a lot of practice in the mini-economy. They've gotten in the "reps." Money is not a mystery to them.

■ ■ ■

I have an ulterior motive in writing this book. It's not just about teaching kids. It's also about teaching parents. I hope and expect that, after you've read this book and tried the methods in it, you'll have more knowledge and more confidence for talking with your kids about money, work, and life.

The mini-economy creates a picture of how to manage resources well toward the goal of living life well. Not only that, but it gives parents a picture of society too. When you identify your values, then participate in your mini-economy with your kids, you get a clearer idea of what you ought to be doing and how you should manage your own resources.

In this book, I claim that children need to practice making meaningful choices about money over time. When they do, they build executive functioning (including self-control and delayed gratification), they build positive money habits and values, and they practice living out their family's money values. They also learn how to align their values, goals, and resources over time.

The wonderful thing about a mini-economy is that it's pretty simple. It takes just a little bit of intentional planning and thinking, but it's easy to start. So give it a try. Make some play money, give the kids (and yourself) a job, work together, set up a family store, help them start businesses, and see what happens. Maybe try it for just a couple weeks. You will certainly learn something about yourself and your kids along the way.

ACKNOWLEDGMENTS

Thanks must go first to my father and mother, Harlan and Heather Day. Dad and Mom, thank you for being models of integrity and wisdom for my brothers and me and for showing us how to walk with Jesus. Thanks especially to Dad for making the original *The Classroom Mini-Economy* book and for supporting me in writing a version for families at home. And thanks to Mom for the many good ideas and editing everything I've written in my adult life.

Thanks to my wonderful wife, Sarah, for being my teammate in this crazy home economy idea, for putting the kids to bed many times so I could go out and write this book, and for being my best friend. I love you and I love that we're a team.

Thanks to Daisy, Calvin, Robbie, and Lucy for allowing your stories to be printed in this book. (When I asked for their permission, they recognized their leverage and demanded to be paid. Fair enough, kids.) Business to the side, I love you and I have so much fun being your dad.

For conversations that added ideas to this book, my thanks go to the mini-economy families that contributed ideas, especially the Bates, Davis, and Latourelle families.

Justin Whitmel Earley gave timely and wise counsel at each stage of my publishing journey. Ward Davis and Panu Kalmi reviewed my psychology and economics content. Many thanks for making the book better. Any errors are my own.

Thanks to the establishments at which I did most of my writing and to the people there who showed me such forbearance and hospitality. Specifically, thanks to the baristas of Alchemy Coffee (Brandi, Tre, and Mac) and to the staff at Common House for brewing me pots of coffee many times during evening hours, even though it was far too late for coffee. ("It's always 7:00 a.m. somewhere!")

Thanks to my agent, Keely Boeving at WordServe Literary, and my editor at Revell, Andrea Doering, for believing in my work and making this book a reality. I've relied heavily on your insight throughout the entire process.

Thank you to my friends and colleagues in the VCU School of Business, the National Association of Economic Educators, the Council for Economic Education, and the Jump$tart Coalition for being a supportive community of academics and teachers. I love how the Econ Ed community bubbles with ingenuity and camaraderie; this book would not have been possible without them. Thanks in particular to my colleagues in the Virginia Council on Economic Education for upholding economic education in Virginia and giving me a platform for this work.

APPENDIX FOR HOMESCHOOLS

Logistics for Making a Market Day

The classroom mini-economy Market Day we hosted at Virginia Commonwealth University was a truly awesome experience. The basketball stadium teemed with fourteen hundred elementary student-businesspeople and two hundred adult chaperone-shoppers. The space pulsed with excitement as sellers bellowed out sales and buyers scurried from booth to booth trying to find good deals. Prices changed regularly as students compared their businesses to others and tried to lure customers to their booths. One student who was dressed as a *Star Wars* Jedi walked up to me, shook my hand, and asked if I liked *Star Wars*. I said "Yes," and he said, "Great, then you have to come over to our booth." It was a clever marketing tactic, and it worked; I bought a handmade lightsaber.

A Market Day is a onetime event in which children set up businesses in a large room, then buy and sell with each other using play money. It's a halfway point between a household store and a real-world market.

In a Market Day, students practice:

- Doing consumer research.
- Using unique skills to make a good or service.
- Deciding how much to invest in inputs.
- Controlling costs.
- Making advertisements.
- Setting prices.
- Interacting politely with customers.
- Setting expectations and standing up for one's own interests.
- Deciding what to do with their profits.

Yes, this is a bit more complicated and involved than a one- or two-family Store Day, but it's a great way for children to experience some of the features of a real-world market.

Let's walk through all the steps of how to set up a Market Day:

- Get other parents on board.
- Secure a location for the market.
- Start your kids on making mini-economy businesses.
- Make a common currency and decide how much everyone will have to spend.
- Do the Market Day logistics.
- Do Market Day!
- Hold an auction.

Are you ready? Let's begin.

Get Other Parents on Board

Does this seem like too much for busy parents? It doesn't have to be. At its most basic form, a Market Day is like a playdate plus some tables and play money. The kids make their businesses at home and bring their stuff to share with each other and all the parents. It's like a small group of lemonade stands but with built-in customers.

Larger Market Days are more exciting, but you don't need dozens of businesses to do one. The fewer businesses you have, the more shoppers you will need if you want it to feel like an "event." I recommend at least eight businesses at a Market Day, which means you'll need to find other families to come on board. This is a reason mini-economy Market Days are so good for homeschool groups; you get a good baseline number of families involved. Each business can be owned by one to four kids. (For classroom mini-economies, four-person businesses are common. For households, single-person businesses are the norm.) The kids can and should shop at each other's booths. If you have two kids per business, for example, then one can shop while the other sells.

Again, the more businesses in a Market Day, the better. This is simply for there to be an exciting "vibe," for the children to be able to sell a lot of products, and for the whole event to be worth it. But if there are a small number of businesses, you can fill the room by having more shoppers—who can be anyone. When I'm doing mini-economy training sessions at the university, I make the trainees create businesses, and we invite the college faculty to attend as shoppers! We pay the faculty mini-economy money ("in exchange for your hard work teaching your students") they can use to go shopping. A room with ten businesses and thirty shoppers feels very lively. If you need more shoppers, invite neighbors, work friends, families from school, and little siblings. You'll probably need to make extra snacks and send out invites to attract people, though!

It is also possible to do a Market Day without having an organized mini-economy. A Market Day can be a stand-alone project that does not connect to the job-budget-store model outlined in this book. I do not recommend this, though. The power of a mini-economy Market Day is that it allows the students to experience how starting a business connects to the rest of their financial lives and particularly how the money they save becomes money they invest in their business.

Secure a Location for the Market

A good Market Day location puts everyone in roughly the same room but gives people space to move around comfortably. I've held Market Days in places as small as a single classroom, as large as a college basketball arena, and everything in between.

Options for household economies include:

- The kids' school.
- A park with shelters—though wind and rain could be liabilities.
- A place of worship's facilities, such as the church fellowship hall.
- A local college. You can network with their education faculty or Center for Economic Education, if the college has one.
- A local business. You can find willing partners through organizations that promote entrepreneurship or personal finance education, such as your state's Jump$tart Coalition or Junior Achievement staff. You can also reach out to community organizations such as the Rotary Club or Chamber of Commerce.
- A children's museum. Reach out to their education staff.

If you reach out to community partners, you will quickly find out just how enthusiastic people are to support an endeavor like a Market Day! Chances are you will also find them willing to donate other items that can support your mini-economy, which you can use to stock your store. In the past, partners have donated such exciting items as sports tickets when they find out what a mini-economy is.

Start Your Kids on Making Mini-Economy Businesses

There are some practical matters to consider in starting businesses. First, you'll want to set a cap on the amount of real money that kids (ahem, parents) can spend creating their businesses. This squelches the "rich kid" effect. Once, I visited a school Market Day in which a group of boys had a "video arcade" business, which was an iPad with an old-school video game shell built around it. The shell was pretty neat, and their booth was swarmed with other boys paying to play. This business was successful, but its draw was an expensive piece of technology. They were basically selling screen time. It wasn't in the spirit of things, and it wasn't fair to the other kids who were selling original creations. What to do?

Head this problem off by agreeing with other parents on a maximum amount (such as $30) to be spent on materials for the business. This forces the kids to create new value, not just bring existing value from their house to the market.

Some Market Days apply a rule that students have to use some recycled material in their creations. This might seem like a restriction, but it can actually be a good way to jog creativity. It also gives resources another use rather than going straight to the trash.

Make a Common Currency and Decide How Much Everyone Will Have to Spend

When you do Market Day, everyone will need the same kind of money. You can't just use your own family's special currency—no one other than the Day family wants to use DayBucks, right?

You also can't have everyone coming to Market Day with very different amounts of money. If one household's or classroom's mini-economy has given out lots more money, those kids would be far richer than the others, and that wouldn't be fun or fair. Some kids might have more money than others because they saved it,

197

but each economy should have paid out about the same amount of money.

When we hosted a Market Day at Virginia Commonwealth University (VCU), we chose the common currency by holding a money design contest. Our currency was called RamBucks (after the VCU mascot, Rodney the Ram). Students from many schools sent in designs for the bills, and we chose the best to use in the market. The winner got a prize, of course.

At Market Day, the easiest option is to give each person there the same amount of money. That goes for both kids and adults. For example, you could give everyone 100 MiniBucks. Unfortunately, your economy can feel less real if everyone is just given money whether they worked for it or not. You can solve this by paying the kids in MiniBucks for their jobs in the week before the market rather than your usual household money. Adults should also have to do something to get MiniBucks. In the run-up to the market, do an extra chore, and tell the kids you're doing it to earn your Market Day money. They will appreciate that.

A more complicated but also more realistic option is to have the kids save up their mini-economy money in your household currency, then exchange it for Market Day MiniBucks. Having kids save for Market Day makes the experience more meaningful and allows them to make choices about spending versus saving.

Here's how you do it. The only money they will have at the market is money they saved in their mini-economy, and perhaps you'll also have a payday just before the market to make sure everyone has something to spend. As the Market Day will have kids from several families participating, how do you ensure that everyone has, on average, the same amount of money while also giving kids the opportunity to save up for the market? In this case, each family gets the same *average* amount of money *per person* to spend. For example, if the average amount each person at the market gets is 100 MiniBucks, then Lucas might get 83 to spend and his sister Clara might get 116. She saved more than he did, so she has more to spend.

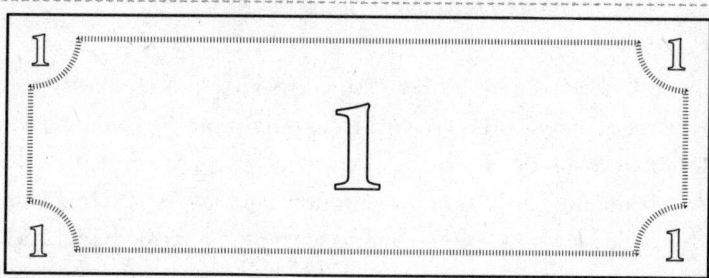

You'll need to find out how much the kids in each family have saved *on average* and convert their family money to Market Day money. You can do this by calculating an exchange rate, just like when someone goes to another country and has to exchange their own money for local money. Sound scary? It's not that bad. Here's the equation:

average Market Day money each person gets ÷ average family money saved = the exchange rate

Here's an example: The Sarasota family uses "FamilyBucks" as their currency. Lucas has saved up 50 FamilyBucks for Market Day, and Clara has saved 70. Their exchange rate is calculated like this: First, take the average of their savings (60). Now plug that average into the exchange rate equation: average Market Day money (100) ÷ average family money saved (60) = the exchange rate (1.66). Therefore, each FamilyBuck is exchanged for 1.66 MiniBucks. Lucas will go to Market Day with 83 MiniBucks (50 × 1.66) and Clara will get 116 (70 × 1.66). If you wish, you can convert the money back to family money after Market Day by doing the exchange rate equation in reverse: family money ÷ Market Day money = exchange rate.

If this seems intimidating, don't worry about it. Only do it like this if it's worth it. You probably won't if you're just starting mini-economy as an easy summer activity for small children. But if you're looking for a homeschool or summer enrichment activity that connects saving money to a real-world math application your kids can work on, then using exchange rates might be a great option.

Do the Market Day Logistics

Get everyone there! Plan for tables, times, lunch, transportation, chaperones, and how to carry things. Make sure your chaperones (parents) get market Bucks to spend. You can tell the kids the parents earned it for their good work coordinating the Market Day.

Do Market Day!

Now that everyone has money, let the market begin! The kids should take turns staffing their booths and shopping. Adults can set a timer to let them know when to switch so they have equal time for working and shopping.

Kids love it when grown-ups shop at their booths. One benefit of adults shopping is that it will give the kids money to spend in the market that they earned through their businesses. Another is that perceptive adults can and should ask questions about how the kids run their businesses. As the market goes on, the money will flow to the kids' businesses, which means the adults will gradually have less money and the kids more.

Hold an Auction

If you are bringing your mini-economy to an end after the big Market Day, holding an auction for some high-value items is of critical importance. An auction might not seem like a critical endgame for a Market Day, but it is. This is because the mini-economy money the kids have earned from their businesses needs to be worth something for the entirety of the market, or the kids will start goofing off. They will sell their goods for either very high or very low prices as the market draws to a close. I've even seen kids walking around throwing money into the air!

However, if they know they still have things to spend their money on, and they know that it helps to have *lots* of money (so they can be the highest bidder), then the money will hold its value until the end of the market. Not every child will be competitive in the auction, especially since many will have spent their money buying other kids' products. That's OK. In fact, it's a good outcome!

201

It once again emphasizes the importance of their money choices over time, and that's exactly what you want.

If you're encouraging your children to make a business or participate in a Market Day, well done! This rounds out their mini-economy experience and teaches them deeply about how an economy works. They will have absorbed lessons about money, work, and choices in a way they will never forget.

STEPHEN DAY, PhD, is a term associate professor in the Virginia Commonwealth University (VCU) School of Business, director of the VCU Center for Economic Education, and chairperson of the Virginia Jump$tart Coalition for Personal Financial Literacy and the Scholé House Center for Christian Thought. He is the author of many peer-reviewed articles about how to teach kids about money. He has helped hundreds of teachers create mini-economies in their classrooms, and he runs a household mini-economy with his four children. He lives with his family in Richmond, Virginia, and enjoys soccer, skateboarding, and coffee shops.

Connect with Stephen:

DrStephenDay.com

INSTAGRAM @_paperrobots

X @VCUEconEd

SUBSTACK @drstephenday